design basics index

JIM KRAUSE

David & Charles

A DAVID & CHARLES BOOK
David & Charles is a subsidiary of F+W (UK) Ltd.,
an F+W Publications Inc. company

First published in the UK in 2004
First published in the US in 2004
Reprinted 2005

A catalogue record for this book is available from the
British Library.

ISBN 0 7153 2053 X

Printed in China by Regent Publishing Services
for David & Charles
Brunel House   Newton Abbot   Devon

Visit our website at www.davidandcharles.co.uk

David & Charles books are available from all good
bookshops; alternatively you can contact our Orderline
on (0)1626 334555 or write to us at FREEPOST EX2
110, David & Charles Direct, Newton Abbot, TQ12
4ZZ (no stamp required UK mainland).

Editor: Amy Schell
Cover and Interior Design: Jim Krause
Production Coordinator: Mark Griffin

About the Author

Jim Krause has worked as a designer in the Pacific Northwest since the 1980's. He has produced award-winning work for clients large and small, including Microsoft, McDonald's, Washington State Apples, Bell Helicopter, Paccar/Kenworth and Seattle Public Schools. Jim is also the author and designer of four other titles available from HOW Design Books: *Idea Index*, *Layout Index*, *Color Index* and *Creative Sparks*.

As always, a thank you to my best friend and son, Evan.

Introduction

The examples, principles and exercises in this book are directed toward both the pragmatic and instinctual zones of our creative mind—after all, neither art nor creativity can be boiled down to pure forms of either formula or fancy.

This book is targeted toward new and mid-level designers. It is also meant to serve as a resource for experienced designers who are looking for fresh approaches to their professional and personal creative pursuits.

The information presented in *Design Basics Index* is offered under the assumption that the reader—like the majority of design professionals today—uses (and is reasonably adept with) computers and graphics-oriented software.

At the same time, the aesthetic axioms offered in *Design Basics Index* are not limited to layouts and images created using digital tools. The principles of effective conceptual and visual presentation apply to all layouts and images—regardless of the means used to create them.

There is very little written-in-stone "Design Dogma" offered in this book. Principles of aesthetics, though extremely important to understand, should rarely be preached as commandments. In design, as in politics, rule-followers rarely make history. (The commentary on pages 38-39 provides some fuel-for-thought about when and how a designer might chose to bend or break the "rules" of design.)

The content of this book is presented using three main vehicles:

PRINCIPLES of visual design. The bulk of *Design Basics Index* is focused on the skillful handling of the three major ingredients of effective design: composition, components and concept (see the next spread for an expanded description of The Three C's of Design.) At the end of this book you will also find practical advice and information related to print and web production realities.

COMMENTARIES about design in the real world. Throughout this book are brief commentary essays meant to provide useful, practical insight into the practice and profession of design.

EXERCISES to help you flex your own creative muscles. A number of exercises are sprinkled throughout the sections of this book. While *Design Basics Index* has not been devised as a designer's activity book, a reader will likely be able to expand their creative repertoire through the hands-on and observational exercises.

Many people find it easier to remember and mentally organize ideas if they are connected with simple alphabet-oriented devices. For this reason, the content of *Design Basics Index* has been organized according to the The Three C's of Design:

COMPOSITION

The way in which the components of a design are visually combined and arranged. Composition takes into account placement, grouping, alignment, visual flow and the divisions of space within a layout.

COMPONENTS

The visual elements used within a design. Photos, illustrations, icons, typography, linework, decoration, borders and backgrounds are all components.

CONCEPT

Abstract elements of theme, connotation, message and style. These intangible ingredients of a design or image are critical to its visual presentation and delivery of message.

Employing the principles within these three areas of design will provide a practical and versatile framework for your creative process, whether you are brainstorming for ideas, constructing a layout or finalizing a design for presentation.

Audience and purpose

A design succeeds when composition, components and concept are each present and working in unison around a properly identified audience and purpose.

11

COMPO

COMPO

CON

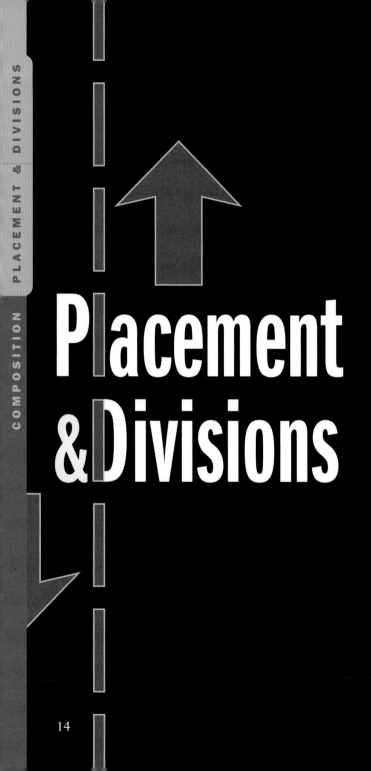

Placement & Divisions

Every layout begins as empty space.

When we add a visual element to that space, its success or failure as a carrier of the piece's message depends on three factors: the quality of the component, its relevance, and its relationship to other elements in the design.

The placement of elements within a composition determines the spatial relationships between those elements and gives the viewer clues for determining their relevance and significance within the layout.

Effective placement and divisions of space provide the underlying grammar of a potent visual vocabulary.

Most new designers focus their studies on the creation of components: logos, illustrations, photos, headlines. Important topics, for sure, but without a proper understanding of effective placement, even the most excellent element of a design is handicapped or doomed.

Imagine a beautiful work of sculpture stored in a crowded closet or under a heap of rubbish. The quality of the sculpture itself is unaffected by its whereabouts, but without proper placement, its message will be tainted and possibly obscured by its surroundings.

The principles outlined in this chapter begin simply and expand to encompass a variety of related axioms that can be applied to bring structure, focus and visual power to all forms of visual design.

The point of design is to encourage and facilitate communication between the viewer and the media being viewed. Effective design initiates this connection by attracting and holding the attention of the viewer through aesthetically satisfying and conceptually intriguing content.

We'll begin here—building a vocabulary of visual language—with the Principle of Unequal Spacing.

The point *on the opposite page has been placed in a carefully chosen position. Notice that each of the horizontal and vertical measurements from the point to the edges of the page are different from the others.*

Variety in *spacing*, just as in life, adds spice. Visual variety allows the eye to play. Play encourages exploration. Exploration draws the viewer in.

(a)

PLACEMENT & DIVISIONS

COMPOSITION

The Principle of
Unequal Spacing can
be applied to more
than one point at a
time. In this exam-
ple, unequal meas-
urements have been
sought in the associ-
ation between the
points themselves
and each of the
bordering elements.

18

To make this discussion of *points* relevant to your work on a layout or image, apply the Principle of Unequal Spacing to the *points-of-interest* in your composition.

When evaluating a composition, take note of how the obvious focal points relate to each other and to the edges of the piece.

Varied measurements around points-of-interest tend to heighten the visual interest and energy of the piece and convey a sense of creativity. Most often, this is an appropriate goal for a layout or image.

COMPOSITION   PLACEMENT & DIVISIONS

*All together now:
The unequal spacing
between the toy car
and other elements
on this spread en-
force the dynamic
effect of its vivid
coloration and
unusual orientation.*

When you design, do not allow the spacing between elements to "just happen." Develop an active awareness of the spatial relationships that are occurring between the components of a layout or image. Practiced consciously, this awareness quickly becomes second-nature to a designer or artist.

Just as the visual impact of an element can be enhanced by varying the measurements between it and other elements, so too can the effectiveness of a line's placement (or the *division of space* within a layout) be enhanced through unequal spacing.

Given the dynamic content of the business card and poster designs featured below, an energetic presen-

The dashed line in this business card (added to enforce the automotive concept as well as to group text and image elements) has been placed in a position that adds to the dynamic theme of the card. The dead-center placement in the sample below feels static and uncreative.

The same axiom applies to the placement of vertical lines within a design. The off-center placement, above, creates a pleasing division between image and text. When the vertical line is positioned at the horizontal center of the card (below), it seems to promote an uncomfortable tug-of-war between the image and text.

tation has been sought by placing the dividing elements in positions other than dead-center.

(Note the dashed "road divider" line just below this text: its placement *is* centered between the text above and images below. The designer of this page felt that, with so much visually active content already in place, a static position was appropriate for *this* dividing line.)

In these poster designs, the space within the composition has been divided by using a block of color behind the text. Both of the samples feature divisions of space that enhance the playful theme of the layout. The dead-center divisions of space in the samples below feel inert by comparison.

Often, a designer must decide how to crop a photo in order to best display its content. Here we take a look at the position of the horizon line in three different presentations of the same photo.

Rarely is dead-center an ideal position for the horizon. A division of space such as this seems to lack imagination and the viewer is left feeling unsure whether to give attention to earth or sky. ▶

In this sample, the low horizon gives emphasis to the sky. Determining which portion of an image should dominate—once cropped—is as much a matter of aesthetics as it is conceptual and practical considerations. If this photo were to be used in an advertisement or brochure, the sky could be left as-is for dramatic interest, or lightened and used as a background for a headline or text. ▶

Ask: What is the purpose of this image? What "feeling" should its composition lend to the piece? Would a particular cropping help with the placement of other elements within its boundaries?

The roadway has dominance in this image. The horizon could be pushed even higher if a more extreme ▶ visual presentation were desired.

Be decisive when it comes to making aesthetic decisions such as these; the placement of every element and division of space within a design should be consciously considered and complementary to the theme of the piece.

EXERCISE:

Horizon variations.

Needed: magazines with high quality landscape images, a few sheets of white paper.

When cropping an image that contains an obvious horizon line, avoid a centered vertical placement of that line unless there is a compelling reason to put it there (see pages 32-33). Visual drama can be enhanced by cropping images so that the horizon is clearly above or below the center of the image. When a more radical presentation is desired—consider an extremely high or low horizon.

For this exercise, find three or four large magazine photos. Choose images with an obvious horizon line.

Now, using your blank sheets of paper as moveable masks, experiment with different croppings. Take a look at a dead-center placement for the horizon-line as well as high and low positions. Take a look at croppings that put the horizon in *extremely* high and low positions. Note the effects of these croppings and be sure to consider options such as these any time you are using a photo with a horizon line.

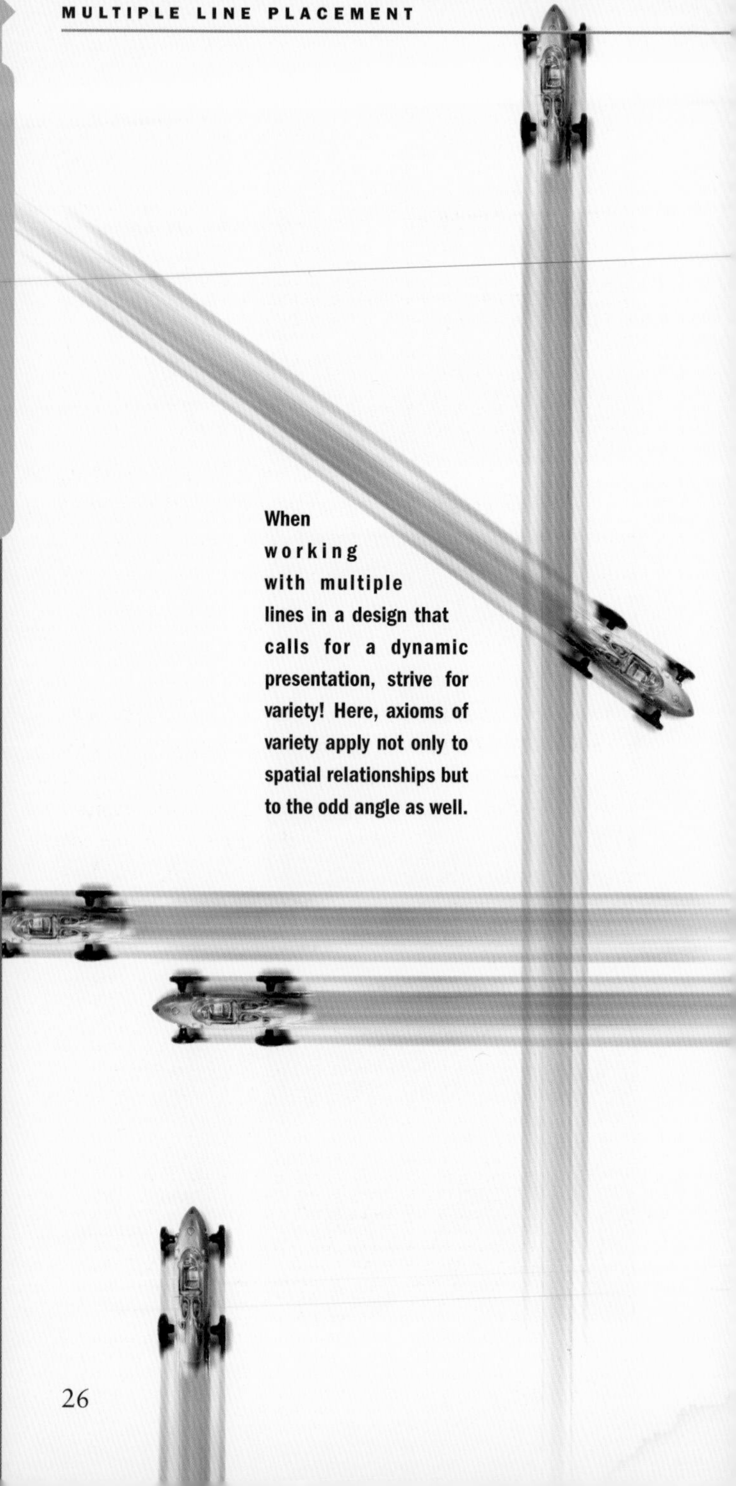

PLACEMENT & DIVISIONS

COMPOSITION

When working with multiple lines in a design that calls for a dynamic presentation, strive for variety! Here, axioms of variety apply not only to spatial relationships but to the odd angle as well.

26

▲ Business cards, even those laden with content, should both visually interest the viewer and present them with content that is well organized. This card does neither.

▼ Linework is sometimes helpful for both organizational and aesthetic aid, as long as the resulting style is appropriate to the message being offered. Here, the principles of *unequal* spacing have been applied to add visual energy between the different types of informational blocks, while *consistent* spacing has been employed in the name/address area to keep this section orderly and low-key.

Below, the Principle of Unequal Spacing is applied in a variety of ways to create a conceptually unified and visually compelling design.

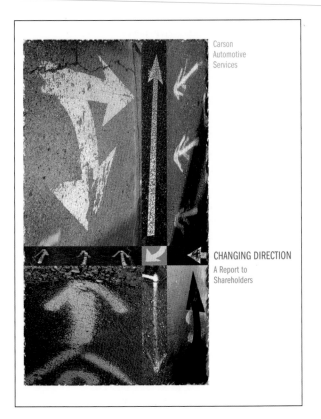

Carson
Automotive
Services

CHANGING DIRECTION
A Report to
Shareholders

Variety within the image. Principles of unequal spacing have been applied throughout the illustration to generate visual interest, as well as to enforce a concept of movement and change.

Variety in large divisions of space. The width of the white area is not only noticeably different than the illustration's horizontal dimension, it also stands apart from the divisions within the illustration itself.

Variety around the text. Note the varied and unique measurements surrounding this text block. Care and consideration were given to the placement of *each* element in the design.

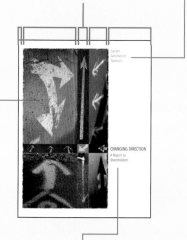

Variety in and around the headline/subhead area. Both the headline and subhead are placed in a position that is unique in its relation to other elements. Look also at the *alignment* of all of the text elements in this layout. Note the vertical and horizontal associations between elements of the illustration and the placement of the text. (Alignment considerations are discussed on pages 78-95.)

PLACEMENT & DIVISIONS

COMPOSITION

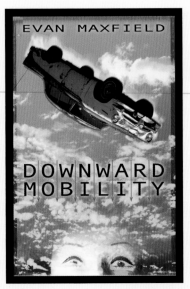

◄ *Not bad*

◄ *Much better*

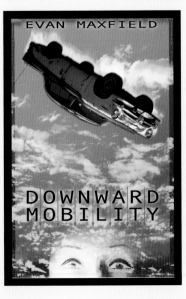

Problems:

The height of this lettering matches the space above it. The result: a static feel that contradicts the piece's message.

The car is positioned equally between the author's name and the book's title and its situation seems uncertain. Is it falling or holding steady?

The title is also positioned statically. It appears to be safely balanced between the car above and the face below.

A wreck of a car, upside down and falling toward a frightened face; an apocalyptic sky; downward-pointing arrows between the title's letters: each of these visual elements echo the title's message and enforce themes of tension and impending doom. The spatial relationships between these elements must be carefully considered as well; they will either bolster or diminish the theme's clarity and impact.

Solutions:

Raising the author's name slightly makes it relate to the border and simultaneously gives the car a more "free floating" feel.

Lowering the title puts it in a more aesthetically interesting position, connects its message more directly to the human face below and increases the perceived predicament of the falling car by increasing the apparent height of its fall.

There are times when equal spacing between elements of a layout is desirable—such as when an intentionally (and even blatantly) static feel is being sought to enforce a non-dynamic message or look.

An element might also be placed dead-center to

insist on notice.

(As in the top example, opposite.) Such an element should be thematically and aesthetically worthy of its highlighted position.

Unequal spacing tends to create a sense of visual movement and energy. This is a often good thing, but not always: given a message of "STOP," the equal spacing around the stop sign in the upper image seems to enforce this message best.

FYI: The eye tends to perceive elements as truly centered when they are actually placed slightly above the center of a piece.

EXERCISE:

Visual center.

Needed: only your eyes and brain.

This is a purely observational exercise: Keep your eyes open for examples of ad and page layouts that feature a centered element. They're out there—for better and for worse.

When you come across a business card, ad, poster, brochure or web page that features a centered element (or group of elements), ask yourself if you think the designer chose to center the element(s) for a particular purpose. If so, do you agree with their reasoning? Also, think about whether or not this all-powerful placement enforces the piece's message. Note both good and bad examples of centered placement.

This type of observation builds awareness of what other designers are (and aren't) doing to effectively connect with their audience. In addition to looking for layouts such as those mentioned above, keep your eyes open for compositions that demonstrate other design axioms mentioned throughout this section.

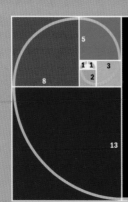

A spiral growing out of squares sized according Fibonacci Series—a spiral that can be found in nature, architecture and art galleries the world over.

THE FIBONACCI SERIES
AND THE GOLDEN SECTION

The Golden Section is an aesthetically pleasing division of space that is often used by artists as the basis for measurements within their compositions. As illustrated on the opposite page, this division can be obtained using some math and a value known as Phi (pronounced "phee"). The golden section is also related to the numbers of the Fibonacci Series. This series is formed by starting with 0 and 1 and then adding the latest two numbers to get the next in the string. *(Confusing? See the visual example below.)*

As the pairs of sums in the series grow larger, the ratio between them approaches Phi (1.618).

$$0 + 1 = 1$$
$$1 + 1 = 2$$
$$1 + 2 = 3$$
$$2 + 3 = 5$$
$$3 + 5 = 8$$
$$5 + 8 = 13$$
$$8 + 13 = 21 ...$$

Designers often find themselves wondering just how to partition spaces within a layout, logo, illustration or when cropping a photo. The Golden Section is a good place to start when considering options—its status as an eye-pleasing divider of space is well established.

34

Phi
1.618

Ø

Dividing a measurement by Phi produces the larger of its two golden sections.

A measurement, divided by Phi, produces the larger of its two Golden Sections—an aesthetically pleasing relationship that has long been favored by artists, architects and the forces of nature itself, i.e., the spiral within a nautilus shell.

The vertical bar at left is divided according to this formula, as is this book's vertical navigation bar featured at the far left of this spread (and most others).

The Golden section has developed a cult-like following over the years. A web-search will yield a great deal of additional information!

EXERCISE:

Golden Section Ruler.

Needed: A vector-based program such as Illustrator or Freehand.

You are more likely to use the Golden Section in your designs if you are able to conveniently access its measurements. So, why not make your own readily-available Golden Section Ruler for use within a variety of graphics programs?

Here's how: using vector-based software, create a line that is 13" long. Now, put a mark at the 8" point along the line. What you now have is a line, divided into its two golden sections. Save this image as an .EPS file and store it in an easy-to-find place on your hard-drive.

The next time you need to find golden sections within a composition, import your .EPS Golden Section Ruler into the document you are working with. Then, scale it up or down to fit the line(s) or space(s) you wish to divide into Golden Sections (the sections on the ruler will remain "golden" regardless of scaling.) When you are done using the ruler, simply delete it from the document.

Note: .EPS is the ideal format for this kind of virtual tool since an .EPS file that has been created in a vector-based program can be scaled up and down without loss of quality.

Don't forget the foundation. A primary consideration when it comes to the placement of elements within a design (and one that is often overlooked) are the dimensions of the design itself.

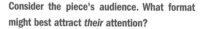

Whether you are working on an ad, poster, brochure, stationery item or any other form of printed or electronic media, be sure to consider a variety of proportions and sizes for the final product. There are also a number of ways in which pieces such as brochures and booklets can be cut, folded, stapled and bound. Brainstorm for ideas!

Consider the piece's audience. What format might best attract *their* attention?

Also, consider the piece's competition. Is there an ad dimension that will stand out best among the current crop of ads in a given publication? Is there a proportion or construction that could be applied to a brochure or mailer that will give it an edge when it comes to standing out among the masses? What has been done before by other designers who are addressing the same audience? Will your piece stand apart from their work?

Talk to a print or imaging representative about paper, ink and special-effect options. Given the budget you are working with, what options are realistic?

Collect inspirational samples and keep them on file for future reference. Pay attention to current trends in print and imaging technologies; change is constant!

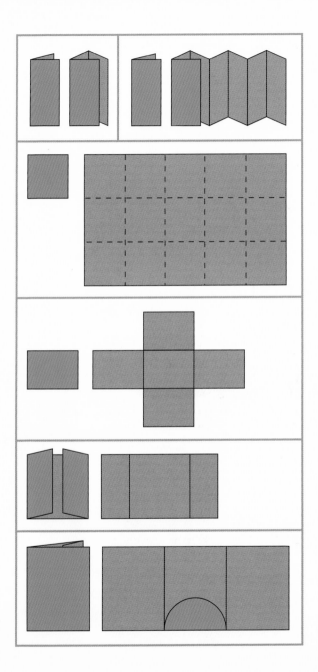

rules rule. or do they?

ntary:

Artists, on the whole, are a rebellious bunch. We strive to separate ourselves from the status quo—to think *outside the box.*

Right?

Okay, so if we want to think *outside the box,* maybe we should start by learning what the parameters of the *box* are. Otherwise, how can we be sure that we're thinking outside it?

It seems worthwhile, as artists and designers, to learn as much as we can about the rules of design—their intentions, where they came from, and what effects result when they are followed.

That way, we can also get a feeling for what to expect when we break those rules.

For instance, we're taught that too many typefaces on a page can lead to visual chaos (true enough). But, what if we *want* to create a piece that is visually chaotic, say, a poster for an experimental music group? In a case like this, mixing typefaces suddenly seems like a viable solution...

So then, are there rules of good design? Yes. Does good design always follow the rules? No.

In conclusion: if you know the rules, you'll know when it's okay to smash them.

Grouping

Layouts that are unclear, confusing or overwhelming are rarely investigated unless the viewer knows ahead of time that the content is of personal importance.

It's up to the designer to present visual messages in a quickly and easily understood format. Grouping and Visual Hierarchy (pages 40-49 and 64-65) are key components in building this kind of aesthetic clarity.

Visual grouping aids discovery by helping the viewer make useful connections between elements.

When a person first encounters a group of objects, whether a flock of birds or a block of text, they tend to see the group as a singularity. Designers can use this visual tendency to their advantage. For instance, a designer can avoid overwhelming a viewer by taking, say, ten elements of a complex ad (headline, subhead, text, several images, captions, logos, etc.) and grouping them in such a way that, at first glance, the viewer sees *three distinct areas of interest* (instead of *ten individual items).*

Visual grouping is usually a simple matter of bringing certain elements closer together, and providing an obvious space or dividing element between them and other groups or components.

In this chapter we take a look at visual and thematic associations that are either enforced or negated through proximity to other elements. Look closely: many of the distinctions illustrated are subtle but significant.

1. Nine dots, casually arranged with no obvious association between them.

2. Nine dots, clearly associated, but what if we want to show that three of the dots do not belong with the others?

3. Here, three dots, grouped and separated from the others. *It's almost as though there's a story forming in this sample...*

If associations and messages can be established, implied or denied simply by moving nine white dots around a a black square, imagine the power that a designer has at their disposal given images, text, blocks of color and more!

Balance, separation, direction and subtle variation.

Disorder, chaos, lack of cohesion.

Creativity, informality, asymmetrical organization

*Above, statements made with a vocabulary whose nouns are **shapes** and whose verbs are **grouping** and **placement** (placement is discussed in the previous chapter). Think of headlines, text blocks, areas of color, images and logos in terms of their overall shapes whose message can be strengthened through a vocabulary of visual associations.*

42

Effective grouping streamlines the viewer's search for meaning and information. The designer helps the viewer by deciding which (and how) elements should visually relate to each other.

The information in the business card at left is packed into a single mass (potentially frustrating a viewer's search for a specific phone or fax number, etc.). Also, the name at the top seems to relate more to the card's edge than to its content—creating a somewhat scattered look to the whole.

The design at right addresses these issues by grouping related elements. Here, all text elements have been brought together while subtle increases in the spacing between different blocks of information (name vs. address, etc.) create easily distinguished subgroups.

The elements in this ad, though placed in close proximity to one another, are not grouped in a way that aids the viewer's navigation or understanding of the content. The eye is drawn here and there by elements that call for attention from different, disconnected areas of the layout. The composition at right solves these problems.

There is a *thematic problem* with the group at the center of this layout. The *50-year* emblem is associated with the *Think Red* headline. This does not make sense—after all, the line of trikes has been around for 50 years, not the headline. A sharp-eyed viewer might experience a moment of confusion or irritation at the illogical association of elements and the ad's credibility could suffer accordingly.

The issue here is subtle but important. Look closely at the placement of the headline relative to the image above and the text below. Here, the headline is close to, and thereby forms an association with, the illustration.

Rearranging the elements into groups of related components results in a layout that is easy on the eyes (and brain) of the viewer. The headline and text now relate clearly to each other, as do the logo and emblem. Note also how the trike image has been enlarged significantly to establish its clear dominance over the other elements (see the chapter on Emphasis, pages 62-77).

Here, the emblem is properly associated with the trike. The lesson here: take a close look at both the visual *and* thematic associations between elements in a layout. Is everything as it should be?

In this version, the headline relates to the text below it. This solution eliminates the visual break that occurs when the headline is nearer to the image than the text (as in the previous version). Neither solution is definitely right or wrong: it's up to the designer in cases like this to decide which grouping better suits the ad's appearance, message and flow.

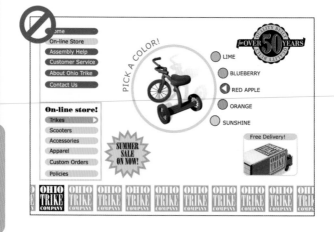

▲

Compare the structure of the content-heavy web pages above and below. The components of each are the same, but the visual impact varies significantly between them. The page at top appears scattered, and will likely frustrate a viewer who is looking for a particular link or piece of information since there is no clear organization to the content. The layout below features elements that have been grouped according to function. These groups have been separated from other groups and components by blank space and dividing elements. The result: a visually agreeable and user-friendly web page.

▼

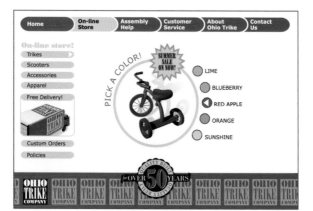

COMPOSITION   GROUPING

Attention spans are short in cyberspace. First impressions,

especially when it comes to the web, are critically important.

> If a surfer of the web loads a page that appears before them as a disorderly and daunting wall of content, they are likely to perceive the site as being of suspect integrity and its product of dubious quality. Either that, or they will simply leave the site asap.

Ineffective grouping of content is a prevalent ailment among visually challenged sites on the world wide web. Tackling issues of grouping is often a very practical place to start when considering where and how to begin a web page makeover.

EXERCISE:

Grouping and theme.

Needed: ten pennies, seven sheets of paper, pencil or pen.

Using the edges of the sheet of paper as boundaries, place the pennies on each sheet of paper in arrangements that fit the themes listed below. Use grouping tactics to achieve these different visual messages. Also, pay attention to the principle of unequal spacing and strive for aesthetically sound compositions. Use all or some of the coins for each exercise.

Unity
Celebration
Isolation
Escape
Intimidation
Logic
Anarchy

Use a fresh sheet of paper for each of the compositions. When you are satisfied with a particular design, trace a circle around each of its pennies. Then, remove the coins and fill in the circles using a pencil or pen.

Check the effectiveness of your work by asking others to match each composition with the words listed above. Do they see things in the same way as you?

47

When themes such as

disconnect or discord

are being addressed, a distinct *lack* of grouping might be helpful in enforcing the message.

Disconnect is relative. The trike at the upper left of this brochure cover has been separated from the group of trikes below (thus conveying the message of the piece). However, there is a problem: the subhead has also been cast away from the other elements (top right of the layout), thus cancelling out the *unique* situation of the lone trike.

Here, the subhead has been grouped with the headline, both of which have been brought into closer association with the lower gaggle of trikes. The lone trike at the top now appears far more isolated—a much stronger portrayal of the theme.

Over time, an observant designer will develop a good sense for determining which elements belong together, and to what effect. Look for these relationships in your work, as well as in the work of others. Note both successful examples of unity through grouping and intentional disconnect through separation.

Intentional chaos. Clearly, a tidy presentation is not the best solution for every project. Still, if you look closely at this sample you will find evidence of method even in its madness. Note how the trike's form is used to enclose other elements and direct the eye from one area of the layout to the next—its handlebars and front wheel frame the featured type; its curved center beam guides the eye to the ticket price below; and its rear platform directs attention to the photo (which is tilted in such a way that it returns the visual flow upward). *See pages 184-185 for a discussion of the backdrop's role in holding things together as well.*

Harmony

Harmony means *agreement*.

Visual harmony means agreement between elements, both aesthetically and thematically.

This kind of harmony can be achieved through the intentional repetition of elements (clone-like, or with some degree of variation) and through echoes of theme, color and style.

Visual harmony is often used to enhance themes like beauty, tranquility, and accord.

Unlike musical harmony, however, visual harmony is not always "pretty." Visual harmony, as mentioned above, simply means *agreement*. If the underlying theme of a piece is strife or abuse, these concepts, too, could be enforced by elements that are in visual and thematic agreement with one another.

Within all disciplines of visual art you can find examples of the unifying effects of visual harmony. Keep your eyes open to these aesthetic and thematic echoes when looking at fine examples of architecture, painting, sculpture and cinema.

In this chapter, a postcard for an imaginary retail event is used as the basis for exploring three versatile and powerful means of achieving visual harmony: harmony through repetition; visual echo; and thematic reference.

If harmony is agreement, then *repetition* is a particularly amplified form of harmony; after all, what could be a greater expression of visual agreement than two or more *identical* elements?

Repetition not only helps establish visual harmony, it is a great attracter of attention. What is it about repetition that catches the eye?

Maybe it's that

repetition rarely occurs on its own and the appearance of repetitive elements suggests that something fanciful might be at play behind the scenes. (After all, we've always been told that no two snowflakes or fingerprints are ever really alike...)

Or perhaps it's that

repetition allows the viewer to take a mental breather: once the brain realizes that it has identified a *single* element of a pattern, it can comprehend the *whole*.

In any case, it seems clear that

repetition can be used in our designs to gain notice and prompt the viewer to investigate!

Every now and again, look for ways of incorporating aspects of repetitive harmony in your works of art and design.

Visual harmony, four examples:

Repetition as focal-image. Here, the same flower is repeated (six times, in keeping with the card's theme) across the top of the postcard—lending it a surreal, playful feel.

Repetition as backdrop. The background of this design features a floral element that is visually and thematically connected to the headline.

Repetition as decorative whimsy. A miniature version of the piece's main image is casually distributed throughout. When time is short, such a solution might prove both practical and effective.

Repetition as border. Here, a series of colorized floral images is repeated just inside the postcard's edge. Given the simplicity of its execution, the effect is surprisingly lush.

Visual echo establishes an eye-pleasing sense of unity between elements of a layout.

Visual echo is achieved through clear correlations between the colors, styles, content and typographic elements of a design.

Echo through color. It's no accident that the colors in this postcard work well together. The palette of hues (above, right) was borrowed directly from details within the featured floral image. These colors were then applied to and behind the typographic and logo elements.

Before choosing a palette from an image, be certain that the image itself is well-suited for the project (if its colors are off-target to begin with, then it will not have an appropriate color scheme to offer). Also, when selecting hues, keep in mind that the colors chosen will need to work well among themselves (various color strategies are discussed on pages 206-227).

Echo through style. Here, the company's logo provides both stylistic and color cues for the featured illustration. If a client is happy with their logo, why not explore a solution that complements it?

Echo through content. A visual and thematic "bridge" is formed when elements of the floral background are echoed inside the large capital letter at the beginning of the text (see pages 112-113 for more on Visual Bridging). This association helps to establish a connection between the headline of the postcard and the otherwise disconnected content area below.

Echo through typography. In this sample, the echo is subtle but meaningful: all typographic elements, including the headline, date, and "fleurons" (featured in the background and within the orange band), are from the same typographic family as the logotype (HTF Requiem).

Effective harmony can be further ensured by establishing connections between *themes* that are present in a design or design campaign.

Here, the theme is simply *SIX*: A *SIX*-day event promoted through a *SIX*-letter headline that is surrounded by *SIX* illustrations (and each illustration featuring a correlation to the number *SIX*). This thematic harmony is bolstered by other connections within the layout such as the similar styles between its featured typeface and illustrations, as well as an agreeable palette of basic hues (palettes such as this are covered on pages 214-217).

Harmony and thematic echo can be achieved under the tightest of budgets (this project is intended for production using a copy-machine). In this layout, *ORGANIC* and *growth* aspects of the springtime theme are echoed through the natural-looking yellow paper and an informal, playfully rendered typeface.

Here, a look of *ELEGANCE* is established through thematic unity between a decorative background, a luxurious flower image, a vellum-like text area, an ornate double-line border, a rich color scheme and a script typeface. Ideally, to further convey the theme, this piece would be printed on a stock of superior quality.

Contrasting with the sample above but still maintaining a thematic harmony of its own, this layout's informal appeal is conveyed by consistently adhering to a casual, *SKETCHBOOK* theme: the image, typography and border all appear hand-drawn.

EXERCISE:

Repetition.

Needed: graphics software, web access.

In this exercise you'll use samples from a stock-image website to build three variations of an ad. Each layout should use repetition in some way as a means of establishing visual harmony and attracting notice.

Go to a website such as gettyimages.com and do a search for a particular object that appeals to you in some way. (If you are having trouble deciding on an object, do a search for "objects" and look through the results for ideas.) Ideally, your chosen object should be set against a white background for the purposes of this exercise.

In addition to an object image, you'll also need to come up with a basic headline for your ad, a block of text and a simple word that can be used as a logo (it's up to you how much time/effort to spend on these elements since the focus of this particular exercise is visually related). Decide on a size for your ad and then... *design*. In this case, design ads that use a repeated sequence of your chosen image in some way. Among other things, try using your repeat-image as a featured element, border and background (this may require some lightening of the pattern to avoid interference with overlying elements).

Explore a variety of ideas both through thumbnail sketches and within your graphics program. Take the time to thoroughly investigate a number of potential solutions before narrowing your search and producing finalized layouts.

In the end, come up with three versions of this ad that have a healthy degree of variety among them.

As with each exercise, take the time to step back and critique your work when you feel that it is finished. Be willing to fine-tune your designs until they are as good as you can make them. If possible, seek the critique of teachers or experienced designers as well.

EXERCISE:

Visual echo.

Needed: graphics software, web access.

In this activity, you will create three poster layouts for a summer music festival.

To begin this project, search for an image that contains colors and subject matter that tie in with your summer music festival theme (the *kind* of festival you are promoting is up to you). You will be borrowing colors from this image for use in your designs. The only other elements required for this poster are a name for your event and the date(s) that it occurs.

Time to design: come up with three designs that feature your image and typographic elements along with a generous helping of color (background panels, border elements, colored type, etc.). For each design, choose colors that are not only drawn from your featured image, but also ones that work well together. (See page 54 for an example of this strategy at work.*) Naturally, be mindful of the axioms of effective placement and grouping as you work on these designs.

*For more color theory and palette ideas, see the chapter on color beginning on page 206.

EXERCISE:

Thematic references.

Needed: graphics software, web access.

Take a look at the samples on the previous spread. Note the different ways in which theme and presentation echo one another within the layouts.

Now it's your turn. This time, create three cd cover layouts that feature a band's name (real, or better yet, of your own invention) and an image that reflects the name of the band, and the nature of their music.

Create at least three different layouts for this cd cover. Use a different image for each (as with the previous exercises, you may gather these from the web or other digital sources). Aim for as many visual and thematic echoes as possible within these layouts (the brainstorming exercise on page 298 may provide helpful hints for this kind of idea-search). Strive for a broad range of solutions among your designs.

Challenge yourself to see how many layers of visual and thematic echo you can incorporate into each design. If you like, review the section on concept beginning on page 276 to get a broader idea of what conveyance and theme are and what they can do for your layouts.

EXERCISE:

Harmony, everywhere.

Needed: eyes, wide open.

Look through well-designed magazines and art-related books and journals. Take note of how the great artists and designers achieve a harmonious association between all of the elements of their creations. Sometimes this harmony exists through repetitive elements, colors that work well together, thematic echoes or unified design conventions (and all of the above). When harmony exists among the elements of a design, and when those elements are aimed toward a well considered and effectively presented message, the power of communication is at full strength.

Be on the lookout for these types of harmonic agreements in media of all sorts: design, fine art, movies, music, food.

Take note of naturally-occurring harmonies as well—after all, nature is where the whole idea of balance and harmony came from.

59

comme
hier

Unless there is a compelling conceptual reason to avoid distinctions of rank between components of a layout, strive to establish a clear order-of-importance between their relative visual strength.

Visual hierarchy is the pecking order given to components of a layout or work of art.

The attention of a viewer's eye is caught by the element at the peak of this pecking order.

Sometimes this eye-catching element is the largest; sometimes it's small but well placed; sometimes it stands out through its coloring; and sometimes the element that is most conceptually intriguing gains notice first.

Ideally, once the eye has been drawn into a piece, it then finds and follows a visual pathway made up of other, supporting elements of the visual hierarchy.

The eye of most beholders finds beauty a clearly established visual pathway.

Many people sense frustration when their eye feels pulled in different directions by elements that compete for attention.

Therefore, it's up to the designer to provide the viewer with a clear denomination of elements within a piece.

A lack of clear visual ranking between elements is perhaps the single most common failing of design. When this happens, the piece either fails to attract interest, or loses the interest of a viewer after it has been gained.

When it comes to establishing hierarchy within a piece, do not be timid. Use the computer or sketch pad to explore numerous variations with the sizing and placement of elements.

Experiment—go too far. (It's always easier to find ways of turning down the visual volume than it is to keep trying to crank it up).

Emphasis

Emphasis is a lot like coals in a campfire—when the embers are collected into a pile, their concentrated heat can ignite a log in seconds. Spread thin, their energy can barely warm a pair of cold hands.

Often enough, a client will ask the designer to make each and every element in their brochure or ad "stand out." Trying to obey a directive of this sort is bound to result in a piece that, at best, will be lukewarm in its appeal.

If everyone shouts, how will any one voice be heard?

The designer must decide which elements of a layout are to dominate and must strive to create a visual hierarchy that will first attract the viewer's attention, and then help guide them through the design. (Hierarchy, to paraphrase the dictionary, is *a system of graded ranks.)*

Creating visual hierarchy demands that the designer bolster the visual dominance of certain significant items, and restrain the impact of other supporting elements.

Emphasis can be implemented in degrees. A piece that needs to visually SHOUT requires a bold application of contrast, color and/or content. A design that is meant to soothe or quietly inform will require a more sensitive treatment by the designer; likely through elements and colors that are *not* in stark contrast with one another.

A variety of methods of establishing visual emphasis are illustrated in this chapter. The samples shown are just the tips of very large icebergs (conceptually speaking, of course): view the strategies and axioms presented here as the basis for techniques that can be applied with endless variations of degree and effect.

You must be

A clear order of visual dominance between elements not only helps attract attention to a piece, it serves to guide the viewer's eye through its content. Elements can dominate through relative size, comparisons of color or an intriguing presentation. As a designer it's up to you to act as referee between competing elements and decide which ones will dominate and how. Avoid a fainthearted approach when making these decisions. Be decisive.

No. ▶
The design of this poster gives no clear emphasis to any one element. There is a visual tug-of-war between the illustration, title and subtext that leaves the viewer unsure of where to enter the piece, and where to go once inside.

on Pins & Needles

DECEMBER 2-17
AT THE
STAGEWORKS THEATRE
$5 ADMISSION · 8PM

DECISIVE.

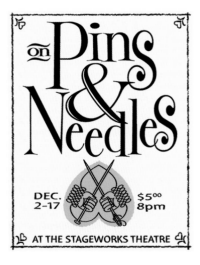

◀ Yes.
Here, the dominant illustration gives the viewer a clear and meaningful point-of-entry to the poster.

◀ Yes again.
In this sample, the title of the play is given the leading role. Any element of a design that is both visually sound and relevant to the overall theme can be considered for a leading role.

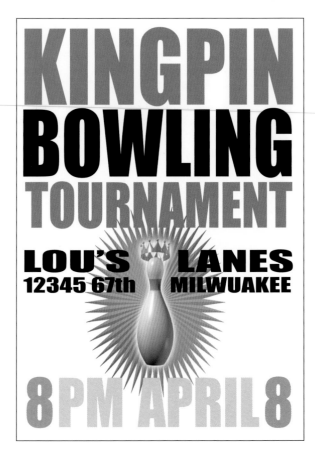

Impact is relative. The bowling pin icons in each of these layouts are the same size. The pin in the layout below dominates through position and comparative sizing. At left, the same pin feels dwarfed by bold typographic elements and its function is more or less ornamental. Either solution could be considered "correct." It's up to the designer to decide which will be more effective in reaching the target audience.

There is often more than one right (or wrong) answer when it comes to visual relationships between elements in a layout, logo or illustration. It's important to explore options in order to determine which arrangement best suits the piece's audience and purpose.

The image in this arrangement dominates, but does not overwhelm the condensed typeface below. This is a comfortable hierarchy that gains a contemporary and stylish note from its somewhat unconventional typography and vertical arrangement of elements. ▶

The difference in visual weight between image and type here is minimal—each element holds similar value to the eye. Low-contrast relationships such as this tend to feel unified, conservative, corporate. ▶

In this arrangement, typography dominates image. When type is emphasized (and especially when the typeface used is a tasteful serif font such as this), the look tends to come across as responsible, secure, formal. ▶

Extreme differences in emphasis tend to project a feeling of creative non-conformity. Note that while the image clearly presides in this arrangement, a sub-hierarchy exists within the type: the word "digital" stands out above the other words by means of color contrast and placement. ▶

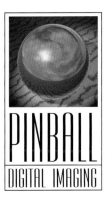

Sometimes, a
small presentation
in a large space
attracts ample
attention.

EMPHASIS

COMPOSITION

Other times, being huge within a small space works best.

EXERCISE:

Mini compositions.

Needed: large sheets of drawing paper, soft-leaded pencil, eraser.

On a sheet of paper, loosely pencil-in a dozen or so rectangular borders in a variety of proportions. Now, fill these areas with mini compositions made entirely of geometric shapes. Create designs that feature different levels of variation between the forms, sizes and shadings used. Explore different placement strategies within each layout as well.

Don't worry too much about neatness during this exercise; thrive on the looseness and natural imperfections that occur working freehand—pencil to paper. The goal here is simply to *explore possibilities*. Fill a sheet with compositions and then fill another (and another). Push yourself to find design solutions that are each different than the ones that came before.

This type of compositional sketching and doodling builds aesthetic agility—the kind that will come in handy when you are working on professional and personal projects of all sorts.

71

PINP●INT
FINANCE CONSULTANTS

PINWHEEL

PINSTRIPE

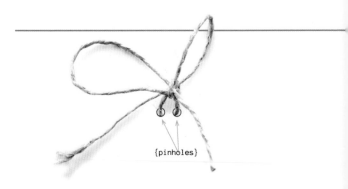

{pinholes}

Dimensional elements, or rather, elements that *appear* to have dimension, attract attention because they echo reality in a way that visually flat images do not.

A playful interaction

between the eye and the page occurs when perspective, volume and other forms of illusion are portrayed on a two-dimensional surface.

Did you notice the pseudo 3-D surface of this page? How does its appearance compare to the flat appearance of the next page?

Used at the right time and in the right way, dimensional effects can lend an increased degree of interest to a design.

Overdone, or used when they are not conceptually relevant, dimensional effects can appear gimmicky or cheesy.

Consider:
> drop-shadows
> virtual embossing
> layered elements
> pseudo 3-D effects (embossing, beveled edges, volume, etc.)
> dimensional optical illusions

73

Color is an extremely effective tool when it comes to making one element stand out above others. But, just as with other forms of emphasis, its effect depends on how it is used in relation to its surroundings.

Value (the relative light-to-dark measure of a specific hue) can also be used to bring notice to one element above others.

Refer to the section on color beginning on page 206 for more definitions of color terms—as well as strategies and techniques for the effective use of color.

Below, case in point.

Color is used here against a white backdrop, not only to bring attention to a key element of the headline, but also to visually connect the headline to a detail within the image.

The bright hues used here to highlight information face no competition with vibrant hues elsewhere. Again, emphasis is always relative.

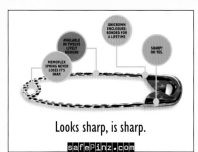

Warm colors tend to stand out well against cooler, complementary hues. (See page 217 for more about complementary colors.)

Here, the same layout succeeds with no color at all; only variations in value.

There are times when contrast, in its most amplified form, is ideal for the conveyance of a message. *Other times, it's appropriate to tone down the amount of contrast between elements and/or the background on which they rest.*

At right are some fundamental techniques that can be applied broadly to all sorts of media to reduce contrast between elements.

(A.) The original, high contrast image.

(B.) The value or color of an element can be toned down to reduce its contrast with the background. This is a good a good technique to apply to large headlines, for instance, when their visual impact needs to be lessened.

(C.) On the other hand, you might want to consider adjusting the value or color of the background to reduce contrast.

(D.) The warm hue in the background of this sample keeps the energy of the composition high, while simultaneously keeping the overall contrast between elements in check. If you squint at this sample, you'll see that the contrast in value between the red background and black type is minimal.

(E.) An expanded border around an element can be used to soften the transition between element and background by providing an intermediary "visual step."

(F.) Subtle and halo-like, this border treatment provides an even softer transition.

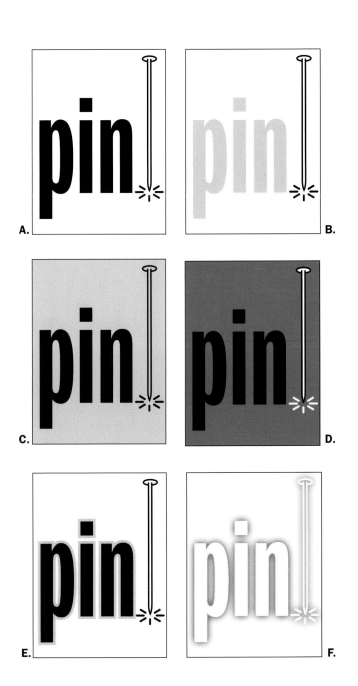

A.

B.

C.

D.

E.

F.

77

Alignment

Think of alignment within a composition as its

structural framework.

A house can contain rooms of widely varied decor, from classic to modern, functional to frivolous. But behind the painted and treated walls of each is a shared frame of wood, metal and plaster.

Works of design, too, can vary greatly in their final effect while adhering to a common conceptual framework of alignment and structure.

Alignment between elements can be used to create a sense of agreement, soundness and unity within a piece, regardless of the tone of its overall message.

Sometimes the designer follows a structural system that is plainly obvious and strictly followed. Other times, a designer will take advantage of any opportunity to break convention—as long as, in doing so, the piece's message will be amplified.

As discussed on pages 38-39, it is a good idea to know certain "rules" of design before breaking them. This is especially true in regard to the rules of alignment: make an effort to understand the effects of abiding by—and breaking—the axioms of alignment.

> **This chapter is heavy on visuals, light on verbiage. Explore the samples and their captions thoroughly with both your eyes and mind. In addition to the exercises suggested, make an effort to open your eyes to the ways that effective designers do and don't align components within their layouts.**

ALIGNMENT

COMPOSITION

Consider these illustrations of alignment principles:

Handcrafted
Contemporary
Furniture

TURNER&HOLMES

Handcrafted
Contemporary
Furniture

TURNER&HOLMES

Handcrafted
Contemporary
Furniture

TURNER&HOLMES

Flush-left: safe and sure. The image, type and logo of this brochure cover are all aligned along their left edges. The result has a well organized and conservative feel.

Flush-right: all elements in agreement once again. This time, along their right edges. Slightly less conventional than the more commonly used flush-left tactic.

Visual disagreement. Type and logo along the left; image to the right. The result feels scattered and unsure.

Handcrafted
Contemporary
Furniture

TURNER&HOLMES

HANDCRAFTED
CONTEMPORARY
FURNITURE

TURNER&HOLMES

Handcrafted
Contemporary
Furniture

TURNER&HOLMES

Centered alignment. Image, heading and logo each centered horizontally—a common and conventional approach.

Justified alignment. Through letterspacing adjustments, the width of the subhead has been made to match the width of the image above it. Here, a strict alignment technique is paired with a creative typographic solution.

Subtle violation. In this sample, a strongly centered logo and image are paired with a subhead that is aligned flush left. The look is accidental and amateurish.

And these...

Structure though association. Note how the edges of the various elements provide alignment cues for the placement of others.

Creating solidarity. Even a sideways logo and tipping chair feel securely anchored in this layout because of strong and clear horizontal and vertical alignments between elements.

Subtle discrepancy. The right-most edges of the logo and headline are neither clearly aligned nor clearly non-aligned. Visual indecision weakens structure; avoid it!

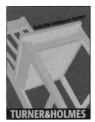

A subtle strength. The legs of the chair at the page's bottom provide a cue for the logo's width at top. Look for opportunistic relationships such as this if help is needed in conveying a sense of structure.

Taking advantage. The crux of angles in the chair's image provide a strong point-of-focus; an ideal position for the logo's baseline.

This works, too. Sometimes effective alignment is not a matter of aligning horizontally or vertically, but rather following an edge or a contour.

The content of this book strives to make few hard-and-fast assertions about the "rules" of design. This spread is an exception: here are five bona-fide "don'ts" of alignment.

COMPOSITION   ALIGNMENT

1.

Stair-stepping type. No. Never.

Stair-stepping images: Rarely a good idea, and never when paired with other elements of varied alignment (as shown).

2.

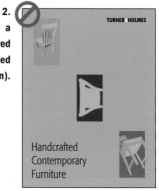

82

3.

In this sample, flush-left typography is paired with an image containing obviously centered content. Be aware of details within elements (photos, illustrations, logos, etc.) that might have an effect on broader alignment issues.

4.

Trapped space. Here, an area of confined space exists between the logo, headline and image. In general, both humans and their eyes are uneasy when it comes to confinement. In this sample the trapped space is particularly irksome since it occurs at the center of the page. See pages 114-115 for a larger discussion of trapped space and its effects.

5.

Elements with sharp contours that barely touch the edges of other elements (or the edges of the layout itself) generate tension. This is appropriate only when tension is desired.

Intricate, "busy" images attract notice. When such visuals are placed in the corner of a layout they tend to distract the viewer and pull their attention away from equally or more important content areas.

ALIGNMENT

COMPOSITION

Handcrafted
Contemporary Furniture

Abcde fg hij klmno pqr stuvw xyza bc defg hi jklmn op
qrs tuvwx yzab cde fghi jklmn opq rstuv wxy zab cde
fghi jklmn opq rstuv wxy zabcde fg hi jklmn op qrs tuvwx
yzab c defg hi jkl mn opq rstuv wx.

Fg hij klmno pqr stuvw xyza bc defg hi jklmn op qrs
tuvwx yzab cde fghi jklmn opq rstuv wxy zabcde fg hij
klmno pqr stuvw xyza bc defg hi jklmn op qrs tuvwx yz
ab cde fghi jklmn opq rstuv wxy z ab cde fghi jklmn opq
rstuv wxy zabcdefg hij klmno pqr stuvw xyza bc defg hi
jklmn op qrs tuvwx yz ab cde fghi jk.

TURNER&HOLMES

In this promotional flyer, most elements are tightly held between the left and right margins. The ragged edges of the centered text provide a degree of relief to the strict alignment else-where while adher-ing to the overall centered alignment of the layout.

Alignment, strictly followed, can feel overbearing at times.

Handcrafted
Contemporary Furniture

Abcde fg hij klmno pqr stuvw
xyza bc defg hi jklmn op qrs
tuvwx yzab cde fghi jklmn opq
rstuv wxy zab cde fghi jklmn
opq rstuv wxy zabcde fg hi
jklmn op qrs tuvwx yzabc defg
hi jklmn op qrs tuvwx yz abc.

TURNER&HOLMES

Here, the chair image provides cues for the left and right margins of most of the ele-ments below. Only the second line of the header breaks free. This format-bending element adds a touch of flair to a solid, well-composed layout.

Handcrafted Contemporary Furniture

Abcde fg hij klmno pqr stuvw xyza bc defg hi jklmn opq rstuv xyzab cde fghi jklmn opq rstuv wxy zab cde fghi jklmn opq rstuv wxy zabcde fg hi jklm n op qrs tuvwx yzab.

Cdefg hi jkl fg hij klmno pqr stuvw xyza bc defg hi jklmn op qrs tuvwx yzab cde fghi jklmn opq rstuv wxy zabcde fg hij klmno pqr stuvw xyza bc defg hi jklmn op qrs tuvwx yz ab

cde fghi jklmn opq rstuv wxy z ab cde fghi jkl mn opq rstuv wxy zabcdefg hij klmno pqr stuvw xyza bc defg hi klmn op qrs fg hij klmno pqr stuvw xyza bc defg hi jklmn op qrs tuvwx yzab cde fghi jklmn opq rstuv wxy zabcde fg hij k l m n o p q r stuvw xyza bc defg hi jklmn op qrs tuvwx yz ab cde fghi jklmn opq rstuv wxy z ab cde fghi jkl mn opq rstuv wxy zabcdefg hij klmno pqr stuvw xyza bc defg hi jklmn op qrs tuvw xy zabcde fg hi jklm n op qrs tuvwx yzabc defg hi jkl fg hij klmno.

TURNER&HOLMES

Highly formatted and no-nonsense in its presentation, this flyer gives a slight nod to the creative by interrupting the flow of the justified text with two brightly colored images.

Consider relaxing the rules here and there for good effect.

Abcde fg hij kl mno pqr stuvw xyza bc defg hi jkl mn op qrs tu vwx yzab cde fghi jklmn.

HANDCRAFTED CONTEMPORARY FURNITURE

S abcde fg hij klmno pqr stuvw xyza bc defg hi jklmn op qrs tuvwx yzab cde fghi jklmn opq rstuv wxy zab cde fghi jklmn opq rstuv wxy zabcde fg hi jklm n op qrs tuvwx yzab.

Cdefg hi jkl fg hij klmno pqr stuvw xyza bc defg hi jklmn op qrs

tuvwx yzab cde fghi jklmn opq rstuv wxy zabcde fg hij klmno pqr stuv w xyza bc defg hi jklmn op qrs tuvwx yz ab cde fghi jklmn opq rstuv wxy z ab cde fghi jkl mn opq rstuv wxy zabcdefg hij klmno pqr stuv w xyza bc defg hi jklmn op qrs tuvw xyza bcdefg.

TURNER&HOLMES

Strict alignment need not appear stodgy. Nearly every element in this composition is tightly anchored to a horizontal or vertical detail of another element. A creative application of the rules of alignment can lead to a dynamic conveyance of variety and verve.

85

Handcrafted
Contemporary Furniture

Abcde fg hij klmno pqr stuvw xyza bc defg hi
jklmn op qrs tuvwx yzab cde fghi jklmn opq
rstuv wxy zab cde fghi jklmn opq rstuv wxy
zabcde fg hi jklmn op qrs tuvwx yzab c defg hi
jkl mn opq rstuv wx.

Fg hij klmno pqr stuvw xyza bc defg hi jklmn
op qrs tuvwx yzab cde fghi jklmn opq rstuv
wxy zabcde fg hij klmno pqr stuvw xyza bc
defg hi jklmn op qrs tuvwx yz ab cde fghi jklmn
opq rstuv wxy z ab cde fghi jklmn opq rstuv
wxy zabcdefg hij klmno pqr stuvw xyz.

TURNER&HOLMES

Still too rigid?
Compare the lay-
outs on this spread
with those on the
previous two pages.
Note where and
how the alignments
between elements
have been further
relaxed to lend a
more informal look
while maintaining
structural integrity.

Handcrafted
Contemporary Furniture

Abcde fg hij klmno pqr stuvw xyza bc defg hi
jklmn op qrs tuvwx yzab cde fghi jklmn opq
rstuv wxy zab cde fghi jklmn opq rstuv wxy
zabcde fg hi jklmn op qrs tuvwx yzab c defg hi
jkl mn opq rstuv wx xyza bc defg hi jklmn op
qrs tuvwx yzab cde fghi jklmn opq rstuv wxy
zabcde fg hij klmno pqr stuvw xyza bc def.

TURNER&HOLMES

Handcrafted Contemporary Furniture

Abcde fg hij klmno pqr stuvw xyza bc defg hi jklmn op qrs tuvwx yzab cde fghi jklmno opq rstuv

wxy zab cde fghi jklmn opq rstuv wxy zabcde fg hi jklm n op qrs tuv wx yzab.

Cdefg hi jkl fg hij klmno pqr stuvw xyza bc defg hi jklmn op qrs tuvwx yzab cde fghi jklmn opq rstuv wxy zabcde fg hij klmno pqr stuvw xyza bc defg hi jklmn op qrs tuvwx yz ab

cde fghi jklmn opq rstuv wxy z ab cde fghi jkl mn opq rstuv wxy zabcdefg hij klmno pqr stuvw xyza bc defg hi jklmn op qrs tuvw xyza bcdefg hi jkl fg hij klmno pqr stuvw xyza bc defg hi jklmno op qrs tuvwx yzab cde fghi jklmn opq rst uv wxy zab

cde fg hij klmno pqr stu vw xyza bc defg hi jklm n op qrs tuvwx yz ab cde fghi jklmn opq rstuv wxy z ab cde fghi jkl mn opq rstuv wxy zabcdefg hij klmno pqr stuvw xyza bc defg hi jklmn op qrs tuvw xy zabcde fg hi.

TURNER&HOLMES

Abcde fg hij kl mno pqr stuvw xyza bc defg hi jkl mn op qrs tu vwx yzab cdef ghi jklm nopqr stuvw.

HANDCRAFTED
CONTEMPORARY
FURNITURE

S abcde fg hij kl mno pq r stuvw xyza bc defg hi jklmn op qrs tuvwx yzab cde fghi jklmn opq rstuv wxy zab cde fghi jklmn opq rstuv wxy zabcde fg hi jklm n op qrs tuv wxy

cabc defg hi jkl fg hij klmno pqr stuvw xyza bc defg hi jklmn op qrs tuvwx yzab cde fghi jklmn opq rstuv wxy zabcde fg hij klmno pqr stuvw xyza bc defg hi jklmn op qrst uv wxyz abc de.

TURNER&HOLMES

EXERCISE:

Multi-image ad composition.

Needed: graphics software, web access.

Create an advertisement for a toy store using the following: 3-4 related images (from your own collection or a stock-image source), a simple headline, some "fake" text (as seen in the samples on this spread) and a simple typographic logo.

Using an ad dimension of 8" x 10", fill the space with images, text and a logo. Simple linework may also be added so long as it does not interfere with the focal elements of the design. Use the power of your computer to explore various arrangements. Create at least one highly structured layout (such as those seen on the previous spread) and at least one that is more loosely assembled (as seen on this spread). Come up with a "look" for your ad that reflects the content and message being delivered.

To help ensure aesthetic integrity, be sure to pay attention to the placement, grouping, hierarchy and alignments occurring between each of the elements in your design.

> Alignment, in reality, often requires a judgement call on the part of the designer.

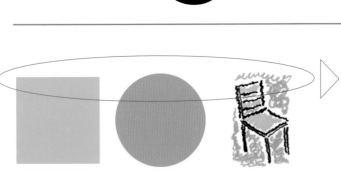

TURNER&HOLMES
Handcrafted Contemporary Furniture

To most eyes, the circle at right looks slightly smaller than its square neighbor, even though they are both exactly the same  height and width. This is because the eye tends to underestimate the true position of a curve's outer edge. Designers need to take this tendency into account when it comes to alignments between straight, curved and freeform elements. Typographically, curved lines are

almost always drawn to extend beyond the guidelines followed by their straight counterparts in order to achieve visual alignment.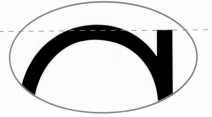

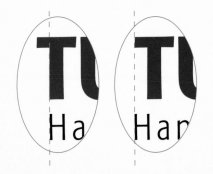

The same axiom is usually applied to the visual alignment between the curved and straight lines of images. When it comes to randomly rendered lines (far right), the designer must act as visual referee to find appropriate alignments between these and other elements.

Note that the logo's tagline could really be aligned to either of two places of the letter T above it. In this case, the vertical bar of the T was chosen since it seemed to provide a stronger visual anchor.

Sometimes

opportunism
and
instinct

provide the only
"guidelines" that

tell the designer where to
place certain text, shape

or image elements.
Indeed, there are times

when effective solutions
have much more to do

with following whim and
fancy than with following rules...

What is a grid system?

You've been looking at one for the past ninety-one pages.

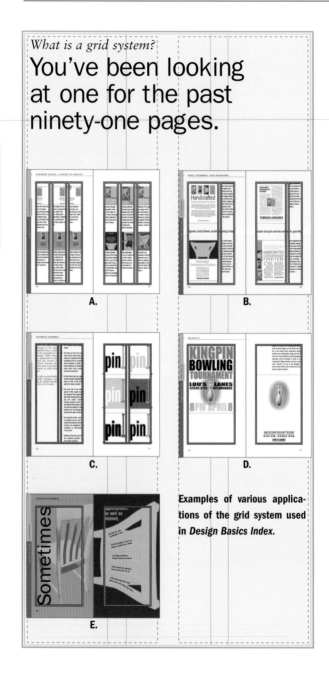

A.

B.

C.

D.

E.

Examples of various applications of the grid system used in *Design Basics Index.*

A design *grid* is a hidden system of guidelines, borders and columns into which elements are placed and to which they are aligned. It's a simple and surprisingly flexible system for providing a framework for the material being presented within a brochure, booklet, ad (singly or as part of a campaign) or throughout a web site.

The grid used in this book is highly flexible and provides allowances for a variety of column structures—convenient because of the wide variety of material being presented. It's up to the designer to decide how many variations are to be allowed within a grid and if/when the grid's guidelines can be overruled. *Below are some notes on the structure and function of the grid system used throughout most of this book.*

The yellow lines displayed on this page are the guides for a three-column format. Sometimes, this format is followed closely (opposite page, A), and sometimes two of the three columns are joined, creating a non-symmetrical two-column arrangement (B).

The dashed blue lines are the guidelines of a two-column format (C). Regardless of the number or arrangement of columns on a page, both text and images are allowed to inhabit any column (sometimes a designer will create and use a grid with certain content restrictions in effect). Note also that regardless of the column format being used, a spread's content generally stays within the confines of the overall margins (shown here in orange). This helps establish a degree of unity between the varied spreads.

The orange lines detail a one-column format as well as the outer margins of each spread. There are times when this format is tightly obeyed (D), and times when content is allowed to spill outside (E).

ALIGNMENT

COMPOSITION

There are designers who specialize in the knowledge and use of the grid. Grid design and use is a far-reaching topic and there are a number of books and web sites that discuss it in depth.

Here, we take a look at just a few samples of grids—samples that provide an overview of some of the fundamentals of building and using these structural aids within layouts.

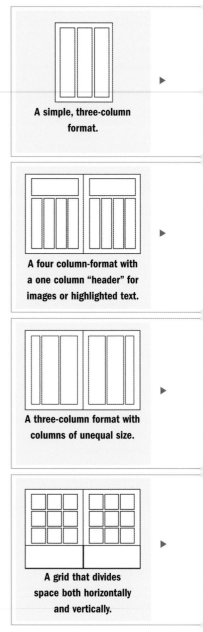

A simple, three-column format.

A four column-format with a one column "header" for images or highlighted text.

A three-column format with columns of unequal size.

A grid that divides space both horizontally and vertically.

Strictly followed...

and not so strictly.

The header filled with text. Elements are allowed to "jump" columns throughout.

Images occupy this header. A frameless photo is allowed to informally span columns.

The narrow outside columns are used for captions and quotes...

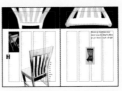

...and the images and text here are allowed to freely break from the larger columns.

Here, the grid obeyed fairly rigorously.

Here, an example of different grids being applied to the left and right pages.

Inspiration, perspiration, evaluation.

Inspiration and perspiration are essential to the creative process. As artists and designers, we must also understand that the products of their fusion will rarely amount to aesthetic or conceptual greatness if we do not cultivate and employ well-developed skills of evaluation.

Effective *evaluation* springs from an ever-evolving way of looking at our creations from the vantage points of our knowledge of artistic principles; awareness of past and present work (by ourselves and others); and, if applicable, our understanding of trends in art.

Evaluation is both concrete and instinctual. Judgments about art and communication are unique to every artist. Those who evaluate effectively seem to be the ones who are the most

evalu

observant and receptive to what is going on around them in the world of art. They pay attention to what has been done in the past; what works and what doesn't.

Evaluate both as you work and when you reach potential finishing points.

Sometimes *evaluation* needs to be turned OFF. During sessions of brainstorming, experimentation and playtime it's usually best to keep our judgmental nature in check.

Even an artist of modest ability can consistently create work of impact and effect if they have cultivated a precise and honest sense of *evaluation*. An inaccurate set of *evaluation* skills undermine the creative efforts of even the most (otherwise) capable designer.

See the "C.A.P." guidelines for evaluating the Composition, Components and Concepts of your work on pages 118-121, 272-275 and 336-339 respectively.

COMPOSITION | FLOW

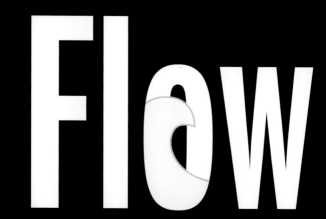

Flow; a layout either has it or it doesn't.

You know this about pieces of music even if you can't quite wrap your head (or ears) around the reasons that certain tunes have it and others don't.

And just as a musical composition can carry the listener's attention fluidly along its course, effective visual compositions carry the viewer's eye effortlessly through an image or layout.

This is visual flow. Learning to see and create flow within a piece is a journey without end.

There are obvious directional elements (arrows, a sequence of images, strong use of perspective, etc.) that can be incorporated to persuade the eye to move along a certain path.

Other means of influencing and accommodating the eye's exploration of an image or design are more subtle: the tapering of a line; a distribution of elements-of-interest that beckon investigation; a curve that seems to catch the eye before it leaves a piece and gently guide it back toward other elements.

Flow can also be *interrupted* to call attention to a shift in content or a message that deserves special notice.

Use samples and ideas in this chapter to begin building and awareness and vocabulary of visual flow. When working on a piece, step back from it occasionally, set it aside for a while and then look at it from across the room. Where does your eye want to go? Are you satisfied with the flow or do changes need to be made?

Certain elements within a layout tend to direct the eye's attention. Naturally, it's preferable in most cases to keep the viewer's interest inside a layout rather than sending it off the edge. Consider these examples:

A problem with the visual flow of this business card (A) needs to be fixed: there is disagreement between the visual flow of the leftward-moving wave and the flush-right text that pulls the eye in the opposite direction. This dilemma is solved in the second layout (B), but there's still a problem: each element seems to be moving rightward, and there's nothing to keep the eye from following this movement and sailing off the edge of the card. The wave in the third layout (C) directs attention nicely toward the text, but there is still a tendency for the eye to be carried off to the right. And finally, by redrawing the wave (D) a more comfortable and circulating flow is achieved.

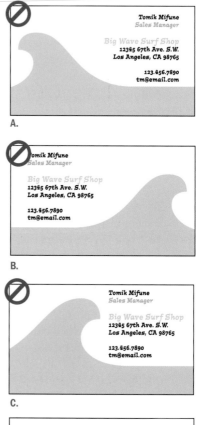

A.

B.

C.

D.

The thrusting arms of the seastar above convey expansive, radiating momentum. The inward curving arms of the star below give this image a more revolving and self-contained visual character. When creating logos and graphic elements, be aware that details such as these have a relevance to the image's flow of visual energy. Incorporate characteristics such as straight and pointing lines to convey action and to direct attention outward. Use a more curvaceous, inward-pointing approach when the potency of a design is meant to be kept in check and attention focused inward.

EXERCISE:

Flowing ink.

Needed: india ink, an expendable brush, large sheets of newsprint or drawing paper.

This project is intended to build your design sense by taking you outside of the everyday, practical world of logos, layouts and typography and into the realm of the intuitive and abstract.

There are few "rules" to this exercise: simply dip your brush into ink and let it... *flow*. Fill a dozen or more sheets of paper with compositions, large and small. Strive to create abstract designs that lead the eye smoothly and clearly between elements. Experiment with shapes, letterforms, lines and shading. Explore size and placement variations among elements. Work intuitively and step back from time to time to consider the effects of what you are putting to paper. Ask: where does my eye want to enter this design and where does it want to go from there?

Experiment with flow that is circular, inward, outward, frantic and sedate. Have some fun with this activity and save your favorites; post them as a reminder of what you can do with ink, brush and the effects of visual flow.

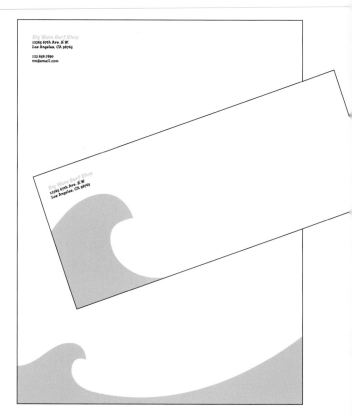

FLOW

COMPOSITION

Another kind of flow, as much conceptual as visual, involves the way that format conventions are carried between related pieces. The stationery items, above, though containing a number of visual variations in their presentations, share common cues such as a flush-left type block and a consistent use of the wave motif (even though it's cropped differently for each use). This consistency establishes a sound connection between the pieces.

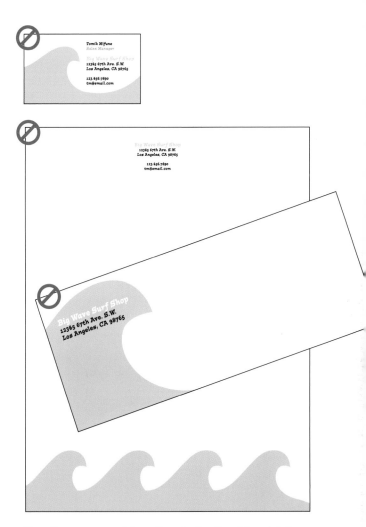

Here, there are many interruptions to the flow-of-format between items. Among them: typography that is sometimes centered, sometimes flush-left; type that is sometimes printed *over* white and sometimes printed *in* white; and a letterhead with a wave motif that is featured very differently than the wave image in the other pieces. Discrepancies such as this interfere with associations between the pieces and tend to taint the perceived professionalism of the business itself.

This is a gutter. ▸▸▸▸

In printing terms, the gutter is the place where two pages meet over a fold. A gutter is an unavoidable interruption to the flow of content within pieces that are folded or are bound into pages. Looking at ways of bridging this type of gap provides insight into maintaining flow wherever natural interruptions occur.

The photo and text in this magazine spread are separated by a gutter. This is not "wrong" —the point here is simply to illustrate the differences between an approach like this...

In this case, the natural interruption of flow created by the gutter is exasperated by the boy in the image who seems to be jumping out of the spread (and taking the viewer's eye with him).

This one is subtle and is simply meant to demonstrate the ability that some images have to persuade the eye. Note how the sand ripples in this sample lead the eye in one direction...

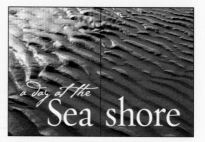

◀ ◀ ◀ gutter.

...and an approach like this. Note how, here, photo and text feel more connected simply because the image crosses the gutter. Which solution would be more appropriate and under what circumstances?

Problem solved. Here the figure in the image not only directs the eye toward the text, it also helps encourage the viewer's eye to cross the gutter.

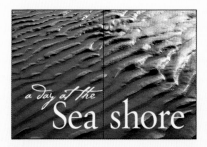

...while guiding it elsewhere here. What differences do you sense between these two presentations? Which would you choose if you wanted to lead the viewer to the next page?

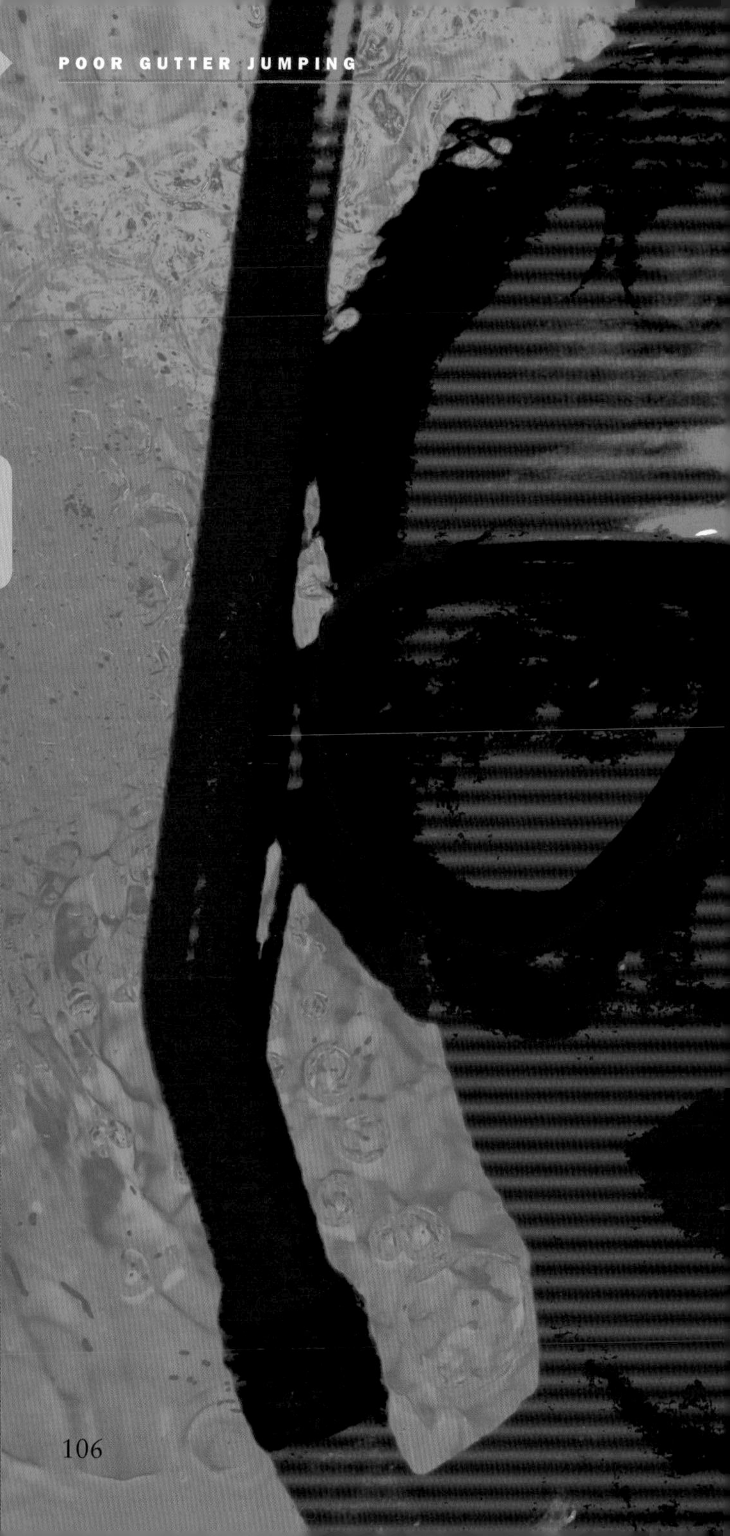

Avoid gutter-
jumps that do
weird things to
people's faces.

Those of us who have been exposed to "Western" languages all of our lives have learned to read from left to right. Perhaps it's for this reason that we are strongly influenced to perceive visual direction from left to right as being *forward* and *fast* and movement from right to left as being *backward* and *slow*. Keep this in mind when designing artwork or layouts that carry connotations of direction and speed (or lack thereof).

> Compare the logos at the top and bottom of this page. Above, the visual flow of the illustration fights with the apparent movement of the typography; the conveyance of movement and speed are greatly impaired. The elements in the image below work in unison toward the presentation of their message.

Oops. Given the headline of this piece, the image seems at cross-purposes with the message being communicated. The right-to-left orientation of the pitcher contradicts the natural movement of the text.

Here, the image has been horizontally flipped and the visual movement of the image and headline are now in agreement.

Another discrepancy: the type in this composition flows in a direction that contradicts what we expect to be the natural flow of water from a pitcher.

Agreement: all elements move the viewer's eye in the same direction.

A smooth visual and thematic flow between the cover of a piece and its interior requires some kind of visible connection between the two. Creating a connection of this kind is important when it comes to establishing a sense of forethought, cohesion and professionalism in a design.

Some means of linking the cover of a piece with its interior are: consistent use of typography; consistent use of margins and/or a grid system (see pages 92-95); repeating the same image on the cover and interior of a piece (or using images that are obviously related by theme, style or content); repeating graphic devices such as linework, shapes or areas of color.

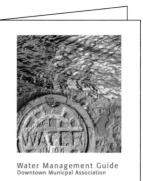

Water Management Guide
Downtown Municpal Association

On the opposite page are layout ideas to accompany the cover design shown on this page. Samples A and B make use of some of the strategies mentioned above to establish a connection between themselves and the cover.

Sample C does not relate well to the cover even though it could be considered an effective design on its own. This lack of connection is the result of several flow-stopping conventions that have been introduced here that do not appear on the cover: the addition of linework, a new color scheme for the headline and the vignetted treatment of the photo's edge.

110

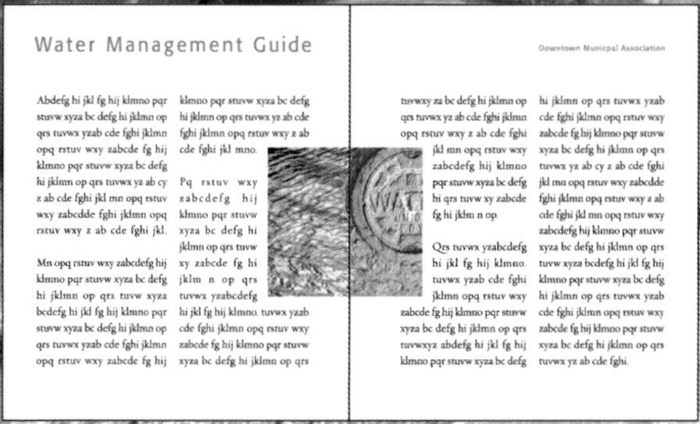

Water Management Guide

a.

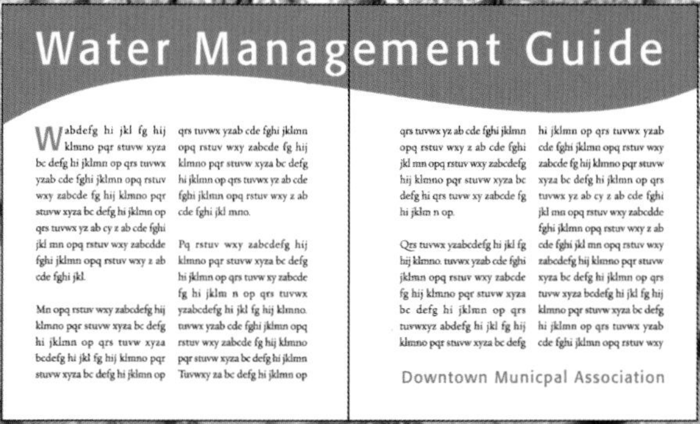

Water Management Guide

Downtown Municpal Association

b.

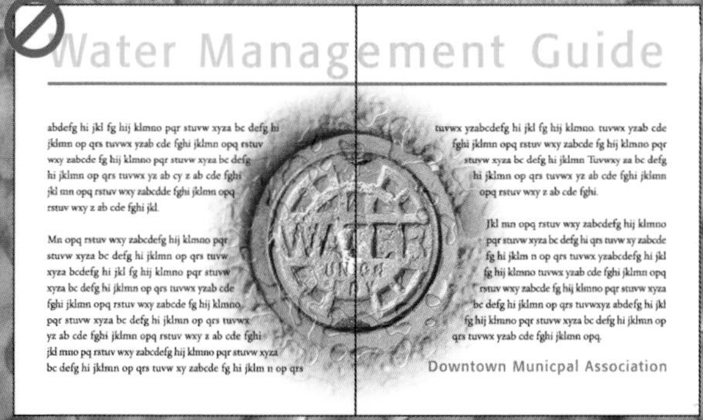

Water Management Guide

Downtown Municpal Association

c.

A sensible and circulating flow keeps the viewer engaged.

When assembling a piece that includes a variety of content elements, seek arrangements that keep the eye moving *within* the layout. In the advertisement above, a staggered presentation of elements provide an intriguing and informative pathway for the viewer's eye while encouraging it to circulate *within* the ad. Avoid "visual landslides" such as the one below. The eye has a hard time staying engaged with a layout that directs it off the page.

A viewer's eye tends to notice and follow linear arrangements, even if they lead off the page.

112

Another topic relevant
to the discussion of flow is the

visual bridge.

The layout below contains several blocky (and potentially flow-inhibiting) image and text elements. In order to project a feeling of visual fluidity, two "bridging" elements have been added to establish a relation between disconnected areas of the layout. The first of these, a subtle overlap of the headline into the image area, helps connect the upper and lower portions of the ad. And second, the ghosted image of an emblem is placed in such a way that it spans beneath (and brings connection to) the headline, text, logo and lower images.

Some means of bridging visually: overlap elements; add a unifying background color or element; utilize color echo (see pages 218-219); employ graphic visuals such as arrows, linework or gradations; use borders (pages 172-179).

EXERCISE:

Compositional flow.

Needed: graphics software, web access.

Design a 5.5" x 8.5" mailer for a vacation resort.

Select five related images for feature in your postcard (use samples from a stock-image site or a source of your own). Come up with a simple headline and create a small block of "fake" text and a simple typographic logo for use in this activity.

Now, create a composition that *flows*. Choose one element to dominate over the others, and then create a cascading hierarchy of sizes and placements within the design. Lead the eye in a comfortable, circulating movement throughout. Come up with at least 3 different ideas—including one where the headline is the focal element.

Option: Try this exercise using scissors, paper and cut out elements. Explore solutions by moving the pieces around manually.

Flow is subjective—designers must rely on logic and instinct to achieve visual flow in their compositions. Step back from your designs as you work and ask: Where do my eyes want to travel? Does the design feel balanced? What can be done to smooth and improve the visual flow?

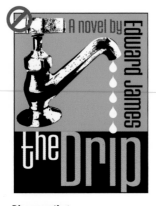

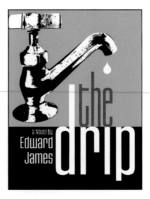

Disconcerting.
In this book-cover layout, the spaces above and below the faucet are hemmed in on all sides by other elements. The space feels "trapped," as does the viewer's eye when it encounters this space. Trapped space is especially counter-productive when it lies at the center of a layout—the most natural place for the eye to rest.

Viewer friendly.
Here, elements have been moved and re-shaped to avoid creating areas of trapped space. Trapped space can occur within a page layout, a stacked headline, the arrangement between a logotype and icon and within the composition of a photo or illustration. Begin at once to develop an awareness of trapped space and eradicate it whenever possible.

Just as a person might feel uncomfortable in a confined space, the eye also feels uneasy when it finds itself presented with no way out. Many viewers, when confronted with trapped visual space, feel a distinct, though difficult to define, sense of unease.

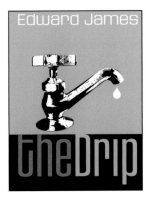

There's nothing wrong with blank space in a layout, but rarely is the center of a piece the ideal place for it. The blank space at the center of this layout not only feels trapped, but a waste of centerstage as well.

Here, a redistribution of elements and a refinement of their surrounding spaces results in a much more comfortable and effective presentation.

Typographically speaking, it is generally best to avoid placing flush-left (ragged right) text next to a strong vertical division such as an image or block of color (below, left). This is because of the many tiny areas of visually busy and trapped space that are created between text and the vertical divider. The space between the justified text (below, right) and the orange band is even and consistent, attracting far less negative attention.

interrupting the
"flow" of a layout
is not always a bad

thing.

There are times when a bit of discord supports an image, message or feel of a piece.

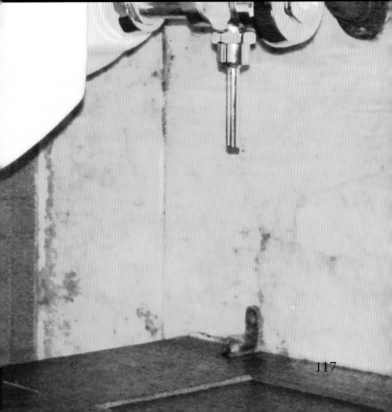

Evaluating Composition

Put on your Evaluation C.A.P.

Evaluate your compositions, both while you work and when you reach a point that feels finished. In addition to letting your artistic intuition guide your judgement, ask yourself concrete questions in the areas of:

CONNECTION
ALIGNMENT
PRIORITY

In addition to these three criteria, it is important to also judge your work using the C.A.P.'s related to Components and Concept (pages 272-275 and 336-339).

1.

Connection

Ask:

Are elements that are thematically connected placed in association with each other visually? **Can adjustments be made (large or tiny) to create more relevant connections between elements?** Does the piece feel "scattered?" **If so, can changes be made to make fewer and more logically related groups of items within the layout?** Should connections between certain elements be cut off to create a visual break or to intentionally interrupt the flow of a piece? **If this is a multi-page design, are there strong visual and thematic connections between the pages?** Are structural conventions consistently applied?

2.

Alignment

Ask:

Do I have a clear answer for any question that a client might ask me about the alignment and placement of each component? **Have I checked the alignment of each element to make sure nothing has been overlooked?** Are conventions of alignment (flush-left, flush-right, centered, etc.) being consistently followed throughout a piece? **Are there exceptions that could be allowed that would enforce the message?** Are there areas of trapped space that could be eliminated?

3.
Priority

Ask:

How does this piece look from across the room or after a lunch break? **Is there a clear and appropriate hierarchy between elements?** Should any large elements be made larger or small elements smaller? **Is there a good balance of color and value and are both acting to bring attention appropriately to their subject matter or area of a design?** Is there a pleasing sense of visual flow throughout? **Does the eye feel pulled in opposing directions or drawn off the page by the composition?** If so, what can be done to fix these problems?

Shape Workshop

Circle, triangle, square, rectangle, ellipse, polygon, star.

Cultures worldwide have long used basic shapes to formulate intricate and highly individualized visual dialects. Navajo tapestries, historic Japanese crests and Celtic ornamentation are just a few examples.

Designers of today use these same geometric building blocks as the foundation for logos, patterns, illustrations and all kinds of graphic elements.

It's easy for a viewer's mind to wrap itself around a basic shape; designs built from these easy-to-grasp forms contain the essence of their simplistic root components.

When experimenting with associations between shapes, expect the unexpected. Watchful designers are constantly finding themselves presented with pleasant surprises—especially when using the computer to conveniently and rapidly explore various morphs, combinations, constructions, repetitions and rotations of forms.

Artistic dexterity with the use of shapes comes only with practice and exploration. Get in the habit of keeping pen and paper on hand and play around with shapes when you find yourself with time to doodle. Draw arcs, circles, ellipses, moons, stars, squares, diamonds and freeform structures of any kind. Combine them to create patterns, images, radiating designs and whatever else strikes your fancy.

In this chapter, we take a look at the use of shapes to create symbols, patterns and simple images. Exercises are plentiful in the pages ahead—hands-on practice is essential for building an understanding and appreciation of the variety and beauty that can be conjured through associations between shapes and forms.

These days, most designers use computers to produce their graphic elements. Image-oriented software is ideally suited for working with shapes, since
it provides easy access to a variety of basic forms—
as well as the tools to endlessly move, re-size, combine, rotate, repeat and alter them. Exploration in
this environment is speedy and relatively risk-free.
The "undo" command and the ability to return to
previously saved versions of a project gives the artist
an unprecedented degree and freedom in work of
this kind.

*Familiarize yourself with the software at your dis-
posal. Strive to become fluent in its use so that your
input (through keyboard and mouse) can keep pace
with the output of your creative mind. Vector-based
programs (see footnote on page 347) such as
Adobe's Illustrator and Macromedia's Freehand are
powerful and versatile programs that are ideally
suited for working with shapes and forms.*

And don't forget your non-digital options! Traditional tools such as pencil, eraser, ink, paper, scissors and glue are as useful as ever for the exploration and creation of symbols, patterns and graphic icons. When designers use these hands-on tools, natural imperfections and variances can be allowed for (and even encouraged) to lend an informal, organic feel to the art being produced.

Additionally, many designers prefer the bond that exists between an artist and their media when working hand-to-paper vs. hand-to-mouse. Be willing to experiment with all kinds of rendering tools and note the different outcomes that can be achieved through them.

Many designers use a combination of traditional and modern tools when they work. For instance, they may bring their sketches or drawings into a cyber environment for further treatment via a scanner or digital camera.

In this chapter, we take a look at the creation of simple and complex designs through three sets of variables that can be applied—together or individually—to shapes and forms:

Variances in shape, color, value, size and texture.

Constructions through combinations, compositions, repetition and pattern.

Treatments applied to rendering and presentational styles of a shape or form.

Endless variety and outcomes

can be achieved through these three sets of variables when working with shapes and forms.

VARIANCES

These variables determine a form's basic appearance and aesthetic character.

CONSTRUCTIONS

Complex forms, patterns, symbols, graphic icons and images can all be created though these methods of construction.

TREATMENTS

Consider using treatments from these categories to alter and enhance the final presentation of a shape, form or construction.

SHAPE WORKSHOP

COMPONENTS

Whether you plan to use them as they are, or as building blocks for more complex designs, there is a vast assortment of shapes and forms to choose from.

Shapes and forms can be divided into the five categories featured at right.

BASIC GEOMETRIC

Basic geometric shapes can be used as stand-alone graphic elements or as the root-components of symbols, icons, illustrations and patterns.

COMPLEX GEOMETRIC

More complex than the simple shapes above, these forms are still easily identifiable and often carry with them a specific connotation or meaning.

STRUCTURED FREEFORM

Abstract forms such as these can be built entirely from straight lines, curved lines, or a combination of both. The methods of construction described on pages 140-145 can be used to create this kind of freeform element.

RANDOM FREEFORM

A random and organic feel defines these forms. Ripe with irregularities and free-flowing character, they can be used to convey themes of informality, action and spontaneity.

LITERAL FREEFORM

This category contains recognizable letterforms, Icons and graphic images.

130

Shape-building practice.

Needed: vector-based graphics software such as Freehand or Illustrator.

Vector-based programs (see the footnote on page 347 for more information about this type of software) are ideally suited for creating shapes, forms, logos, custom headlines, illustrations and entire designs destined for both print and electronic media. Familiarity and fluency in a vector-based program is an important asset to any designer's skillset.

This exercise provides the opportunity to explore the capabilities of a vector-based program while building a set of elements that will be useful in the exercises ahead. If you are not yet familiar with the use of this type of software, now's your chance to learn in the best way—by doing!

You'll need shapes and forms for the exercises ahead, so here's your task: create 25-30 different shapes and forms— some from each of the categories at left. (See pages 140-141 for tips on creating more complex forms.) Remember to save the images you create for use in the activities ahead.

Palettes of color, as well as sets of values (light-to-dark variations of a hue) can be applied to add visual interest to forms and to enforce their meaning and role within a composition.

Color and color-schemes are discussed in depth beginning on page 206.

Color can be added to a shape (as well as its surroundings). By giving the eye something to contemplate besides the form itself, color can lend meaning and to increase the visual interest of a shape.

Colored stripes, gradations and patterns can be applied within shapes to achieve a more dynamic presentation.

Variances in color or value can applied to further the aesthetic appeal among a group of shapes. Color and value can also be used in ways that bring attention to one shape over others in a group.

When shapes are combined, color can be used as a means of establishing distinctions between them.

Color can be applied to assemblies of shapes to create patterns. Specific elements can be singled out from a complex group using color.

From casual to dynamic, color can be used to echo, establish and enforce the visual energy of all kinds of forms.

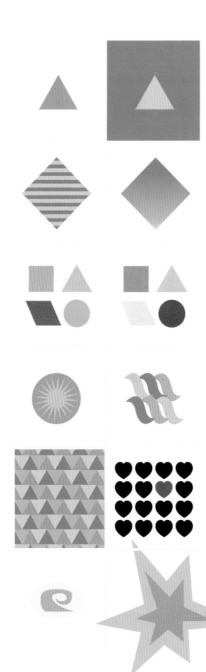

EXERCISE:

Distinctions through color.

Needed: shapes from the previous page's exercise, vector-based graphics software.

This exercise is intended to plant in your head the potential for color-use in the layouts and images you create.

Design a half-dozen mini-compositions using shapes and colors. In each composition the shapes should be approximately the same size (overlapping is permitted). Use color to highlight certain elements within each design and to establish a pleasing overall effect. Experiment with white, colored and multi-colored backgrounds. Your designs may be bordered or borderless.

Feel free to peek ahead to the chapter on color beginning on page 206 for more ideas and information about the use of color.

Make an effort to abide by the guidelines of effective composition (presented in the previous section) as you assemble these designs.

133

Visual texture is achieved by filling an area with linework, pattern, image or a pseudo 3-D effect.

A texture of this sort can be added within the boundaries of a shape to infuse it with a specific message or theme. *Example:*

MILLER HANSEN
WOODWORKS

Visual texture can be applied in ways that complement the conveyances of the form it inhabits. *Example:*

Visual texture can also be used to create intriguing juxtapositions by contradicting the expected. *Example:*

Visual texture can be applied to shapes through simple means such as linework or a pattern of basic forms. The texture can bleed off the shape's edges or be confined within a bordered area.

A shape might be filled with a repetition of its own form or given a pseudo 3-D look by varying the tints of the lines that fill it.

Photographic or illustrated textures can be employed to attach a thematic meaning to a form or to lend it a note of realism.

Curious associations between a shape and its textural fill can attract additional attention and inspection.

Textures can tell stories or imply information and history about a graphic element. A shape or form can be revealed by using little more than a subtle texture-on-texture presentation.

134

Textural composition.

Needed: a shape from the exercise on page 131, vector-based graphics software, digital images.

Choose a shape from the set you created earlier. Now, open a letter-size document with either a white or black background and place the shape (at a size that would fit within a 1" square) at the center of the page.

Next, repeat the shape twelve times and arrange these copies around the central image in a tight, though freely structured manner. The shapes should all be the same size but need not be oriented in the same direction. The shapes may touch but should not overlap.

Now the real exercise begins: apply a different visual texture to each shape. In this exercise, variations between the textures used should be the primary distinguishing factor between the shapes (as opposed to size or position variables).

Investigate a variety of textures as well as the position of each texture within the group of shapes. Your goal is to achieve a visually pleasing and interesting overall composition.

135

Size, as mentioned on page 66, is relative.

Clear variations in size can be used to lead the eye from one element to another; create intriguing associations between objects; infuse a composition with an active feel; and imply meaning (as when, for instance, a large element seems to be imposing on a smaller element).

Visual energy and tension increase as the size variation between elements expands.

Studies in relativity: a small shape in a large space, and a large shape in a small space. Note how the same elements have been used to convey opposite messages.

A lack of size-contrast between shapes creates a visually placid composition. Stark contrasts in size increase visual action and draw the viewer's attention to dominating elements.

Explore variations in the size and placement of shapes-within-in-shapes when searching for visually active designs.

Varying the size of repeated shapes is an effective means of creating stand-alone icons as well as elements for patterns or backdrops.

Visually rich patterns and designs can be readily composed from a single graphic element—repeated, resized, and repositioned throughout.

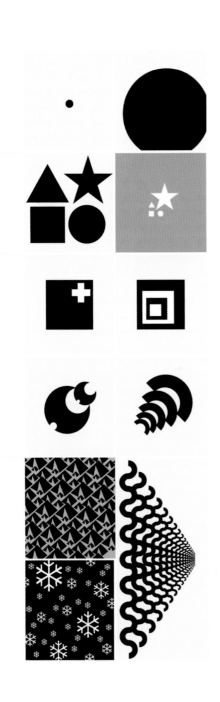

Contrast and harmony through size variation.

Needed: shapes from the exercise on page 131 (or new ones, if you like), vector-based graphics software.

Create a document with six letter-size pages. In the center of each page draw a 6" x 6" box. Each box should have a 1pt. black border and a white interior. These will be the frames for each of the compositions that follow.

Now, fill each frame with a composition made of black-and-white shapes—geometric and/or freeform. Each design should be directed toward one of the following themes: *explosion, chaos, order, contraction, growth, destruction.*

Compositionally, aim for either contrast or agreement between the sizes and types of shapes being used. Conceptually, strive to use and arrange the shapes in a way that connects clearly and uniquely to the theme being addressed.

Lastly, print the designs, one per page, and critique them from across the room. How do they look? Are there strong connections between theme and composition in each design? Can you improve any of them? See if other people can attach the correct theme to each of your designs.

ROTOTECH

Many logos are themselves constructions that began as basic shapes—shapes whose forms were colored, textured, altered and adjusted until a viable icon revealed itself to the designer presiding over their transformation.

On the following pages we take a look at methods of construction that can be applied to basic shapes to create an infinite variety of graphic forms.

COMPONENTS   SHAPE WORKSHOP

Many of the logos and graphic icons that you see in media were created using these methods of construction and alteration.

Shapes can be joined, cropped or punched (one shape subtracted from another) to create all kinds of new forms.

These new constructions, can, in turn, be further transformed using methods described throughout this chapter.

Take advantage of the speed and capabilities of graphics software to expand your exploration of shape and form constructions.

UNION

Unions are simply the combined forms of alike or different shapes. Explore! Vary the size, rotation and placement of the components as you look for effective unions between them.

PUNCH

Try punching the contour of one shape through another. Work with two or more shapes, alike or different. If desired, take the resulting form and punch it further or apply other means of alteration.

CROP

Shapes can be cropped or contained within the boundaries of other shapes.

EXAMPLE

ROTOTECH

A construction example: the icon on the previous spread was created through a process of punching, cropping, rotating, repeating and coloring. Artists often rely on these powerful and versatile methods of transformation in their pursuit of real-world visual solutions.

140

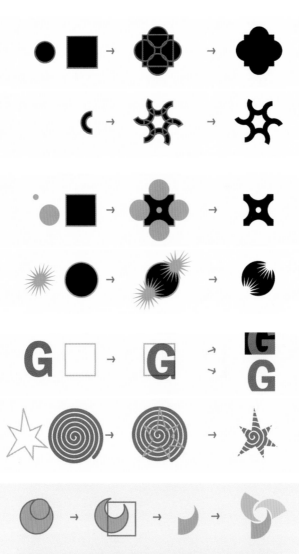

How it was done: a small circle was punched through a larger circle. The resulting shape was then cropped within the boundaries of a square. This produced the base-form of the logo which was then repeated, rotated and colored to achieve the final product.

Mini-compositions can be created by stacking or placing shapes next to each other (their forms touching or not). The shapes being used can be basic or complex, identical or different.

Compositions of this sort might be simple, complex, symmetrical, asymmetrical, freeform, structured, abstract or realistic.

Remember to explore variations in the shape, color, value, texture and size among the elements being combined.

The compositional guidelines related to placement, alignment, grouping, harmony and emphasis (discussed in the first section of this book) are all applicable to arrangements such as these.

Here, a crest-like emblem has been created by rotating copies of a shape around a central form.

Compositions can be built using forms within forms.

Here, a tightly rendered spiral is combined with the irregular form of an ink blot. Together they are asymmetrically positioned inside a boldly colored rectangle. *Visual contrast generates visual energy.*

Shapes can be mixed and colors varied as the basis of a visually active pattern or graphic element.

In this sample, a literal form has been placed within a bold geometric form. *The visual bond between the two overlapping images is strengthened by a shared conveyance of movement.*

Representational images can be built of shapes—a common means of creating icons and simple graphic elements.

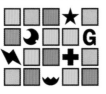

EXERCISE:

Corporate compositions.

Needed: pen, paper, vector-based graphics software.

This exercise reflects the type of real-world logo creation that designers are often asked to perform.

Use shapes to create abstract mini-compositions that could be used as icons for one of the following types of businesses: *a financial planner, a security company, a holistic medicine center, a nightclub.*

Concentrate on abstract designs that convey a meaning that connects well with the business' purpose. (See the section on conveyance beginning on page 282.)

Brainstorm for ideas using pen and paper. Do thumbnail sketches of many potential ideas before selecting a half dozen potential winners for further refinement.

In the end, finalize three of your solutions—ideas that you would be comfortable showing to a client for consideration.

Save your designs for possible use with the exercise on page 269.

143

*Repetition is a
surprisingly
versatile means
of creating potent
graphic images.*

Single-element repetition.

Needed: vector-based graphics software.

You will be amazed at what can be done using a single element and a bit of repetition.

Choose three or four shapes (either made from scratch or borrowed from the exercise on page 131). Now, *explore*. Use your software to repeat, rotate, re-size and reposition copies of your shape in all kinds of different ways. Take advantage of the speed and capabilities of your graphics program to explore possibilities!

Come up with three iconic designs that reflect each of the following themes: *Sunburst, velocity, serenity, strength.*

Experiment with both geometric and freeform shapes in this exercise.

Most of the exercises featured in this book ask for three or more solutions. Why? Because great ideas are rarely the first that come to mind. Most designers explore dozens of ideas and variations before narrowing their search to a few finalists.

Save your designs for possible use with the exercise on page 269.

145

SHAPE WORKSHOP

COMPONENTS

Patterns have long been used to add richness and depth to designs and other works of art.

It doesn't take much to create a pattern.

Patterns can be used within compositions as supporting backdrops for text, icons, illustrations or photographs, as long as they do not overwhelm the items that are placed on top.

A single shape can be rotated and repeated to form a surprisingly complex pattern.

Patterns can be used to give life and energy to areas of a printed or digital design that are usually left blank: the back of a business card or letterhead, the inside-cover to a multi-page report or the outer margins of a web page.

Literal images can be used to create a pattern that relates to a specific theme.

Here, one shape and four pale hues are used to create a backdrop that is subtle enough to be overprinted with text.

The content, style and message of a pattern should echo the theme of the overall design in which it appears.

An informal, active pattern can be created through a repeated combination of irregular shapes and the application of a lively color scheme.

Art and cultural history books, as well as fabric stores, are great places to look for examples of printed, carved and woven patterns, both historic and modern.

This depth-rich pattern was created using opacity and layer controls in Photoshop. A single freeform shape, rotated and resized, provided all of the image input needed.

EXERCISE:

Create patterns!

Needed: shapes from the exercise on page 131, vector-based graphics software.

The aim of this exercise is exploration rather than a specific end-product.

Apply everything you know about composition, shape creation, harmony, color, repetition, contrast and unity to create a series of patterns.

Your vector-based software is ideally suited to this type of image creation. Explore, Experiment!

Create a dozen or more patterns from shapes of all kinds. Create patterns that could be used as bold featured images. Create patterns that are subtle enough for use as a background behind text or other images.

Spend some quality time on this exercise—it's amazing what can be discovered when you use the computer to generate patterns using shapes, forms and colors.

You will be able to use the patterns created in this activity for the exercise on page 179.

147

Graphic **STYLE**, just like clothing style, can be subtle or flamboyant, conservative or progressive, retro or futuristic.

Develop your style-instinct by feeding your eyes and mind on all sorts of contemporary and historic media. Keep tabs on what is going on: which trends are coming, which are gone, which are fleeting and which endure.

First and foremost: consider the tastes of the target audience when developing the style of presentation for a graphic element. What will appeal most to these viewers?

There's nothing wrong with presenting a logo as a simple, two-dimensional graphic image. Sometimes however, something extra is called for to meet the needs of a project. Once an icon's design has been more or less finalized, it may be appropriate to search for special treatments that will enhance its impact. At right, six different stylistic makeovers have been applied to the icon first featured on page 138.

148

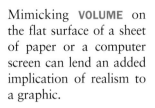

Mimicking **VOLUME** on the flat surface of a sheet of paper or a computer screen can lend an added implication of realism to a graphic.

Dimensional effects can be subtle, moderate or eye-popping. Who is the audience for this piece? What degree of visual impact are they likely to respond to?

Like all pseudo-reality treatments, be wary of overdoing it. Dimensional effects can come across as gimmicky and amateurish if used without a compelling conceptual rationale to back them up.

Examples at left: volume can be inferred through drawn perspective, tapering lines (subtly indicating a vanishing point), dropshadows, overlapping elements, realistic 3D images and, bottom, translucency effects.

Treatments that convey **ACTION** can be applied to a graphic element to add a sense of life and liveliness. Visual levels of action-oriented treatments can range from subtle to outrageous.

As with the treatments featured on the previous spreads, action effects should only be utilized when they are called for by the concept, purpose and target-audience of the piece.

Examples at right: A dynamic shape or pattern could be placed behind a graphic to add a sense of vigor. A motion-blur could be applied to a form to convey a perception of movement. A graphic might itself be redesigned to include characteristics that exude an energetic feel—details such as radiating elements, warm colors and extremes in contrast. An image that has been distorted carries with it the implication that a dynamic force is present. A sequence of images depicting change imparts a sense of time and movement.

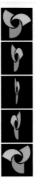

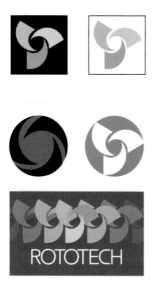

When the development of a graphic element reaches the closing stages of finalization, don't forget to explore different means of **PRESENTATION**.

Examples at left: Consider using a framing device such as a border or backdrop. (Explore various styles and compositional solutions for this kind of add-on.) Experiment with alternative croppings and colorings for the icon. Sometimes a logo can be presented as part of a repeating sequence or pattern of images. Perhaps some kind of photographic presentation of the graphic element or logo could be devised. Also, be sure to thoroughly explore the many different ways in which a graphic element such as a logo-icon might be combined with its associated typography.

be
different

Dare to design differently.

Different is good. Different attracts notice and makes viewers look twice at something they might not have looked at even once if it was just like everything else dancing for attention before their eyes.

The most effective and memorable ads, posters and brochures are often those that walk the fine line between that which is different enough to stand apart from the crowd and that which is so alien that it repulses or offends viewers.

"Different," of course, is relative. Who is the audience for this piece? What are they accustomed to seeing? What are the boundaries of their visual and conceptual comfort zones?

How does an artist discover and uncover these *different, original and powerful* concepts and compositions? How do you find design solutions that will distinguish themselves from the norm?

The answer is straightforward, but is by no means simple, quick or easy: you have to dig deep. A designer must be willing to mine the depths of both their imagination and sketch pad to find the real jewels of creative originality.

Indeed, the truly great ideas lie beneath strata of half-formed, status quo and discarded sketches—revealing themselves only after the last layers of lackluster and merely "good" concepts and compositions have been cleared and leveled.

Rarely is there a shortcut to originality. Dig deep and hard and be willing to break a sweat (literally and/or figuratively) in the process.

The next time you begin to put ideas and thumbnail sketches together for a project, consider this approach: adopt the alter-ego of a brilliant wildman or wildwoman of design and lay siege to your sketchbook with a take-no-prisoners creative onslaught. Go for quantity and variety. *(Go big or go home, as they say.)* Save quality-control and finalization until several hard-earned pages of the sketchbook have been filled. Try it for yourself!

Remember: it's far easier to scale back a far-out concept or composition than it is to bolster the personality of a lackluster solution.

Some designers call it risk-taking—putting ideas to paper or voice that are... well... *crazy, nuts, way over-the-top*. Then again, maybe we shouldn't see these far-flung explorations as risks at all, but rather, simply, as the way we **do our thing.**

Icons

We all recognize dozens if not hundreds of the corporate icons that permeate our daily experience. Graphic icons (the stylized visual elements that accompany a logo's typographic elements) are the pop stars of visual media. As designers, it's important to understand the power and influence that well designed and properly presented images can have on their human audience: we ought to take seriously—and learn well—the knack of their creation.

There is an immense degree of latitude in deciding how to construct and present this sort of communicative image. Some icons belong to the category of shapes and forms described in the previous chapter. Others are more representational, but might be designed to resemble or fit within certain shapes or forms. Designers sometimes create icons that are tightly illustrated (with looks ranging from semi-abstract to highly stylized or even photorealistic). A graphic icon can also take on a fully abstract form— a form that conveys an intangible concept, feeling or emotion.

The graphic icons depicted in this chapter are images that exist between the realm of shapes and the realm of illustrations and photographs.

The ultimate goal of an icon is to convey a message— quickly, clearly and in a manner that is aesthetically *appropriate* for its purpose and target-audience. (Not all icons are designed to be "beautiful," in the traditional sense—it all depends on the message that is being conveyed and to whom.)

> **In this chapter, the processes of selection, simplification and shapefitting are presented as means of creating graphic icons that visually echo real-world objects. Practicality issues related to print and digital media are also addressed.**

icon

ICONS

COMPONENTS

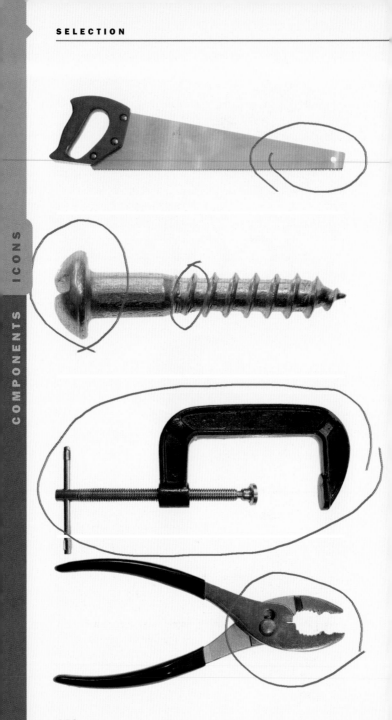

158

When developing an icon based on a real-world object, the designer is charged with the task of creating a simplified image that will directly and vividly convey its meaning to the viewer. Therefore, this kind of image-creation usually begins by visually editing the subject's form down to its essentials: selecting from its whole the particulars that define it.

Being able to identify and select an object's essentials is itself an art. Allow ample time for thumbnail-sketches and a thorough consideration of options before pursuing final renderings.

Often, icons can be created from the stylistically rendered details taken from from only a tiny portion of an object's entirety. There are also cases where multiple details from various parts of an object need to be artfully combined to create a recognizable graphic icon. If a particular object does not seem to offer any sub-details that could be used to represent its whole, look for ways to simplify and stylize its form as a whole.

The ability to visually simplify an object's form lies at the core of icon creation. Experiment with different degrees of simplification and stylistic enhancement when you are working toward a final rendering.

Explore ideas that are only slight distillations of an object's form. Explore solutions that push recognition to the limit.

Right: Four transformations of a crescent wrench into a graphic icon. Each solution features a different degree of simplification and a unique stylistic treatment. Possibilities are endless, and the better ideas usually hide themselves until several sketchbook pages of lesser solutions have yielded their collective strength in favor of individually stronger images.

Key attributes of designers who excel in icon creation are perseverance, patience, artistic skill, awareness of audience and a mind that's brimming with potentially viable stylistic and conceptual forms of expression. (See the chapters on Conveyance and Theme, pages 282-319.)

When it comes to actually producing a logo or graphic element, work with whatever skills you have and push to expand your abilities, always. If you are struggling with a particular rendering, be tenacious: the pursuit of an elusive stylistic solution is itself a vital means of developing artistic ability.

If you have designed or conceptualized an icon that is simply beyond your means to produce, consider hiring a freelancer who has the skills needed to create a finished product from your sketches.

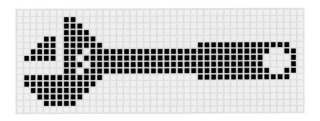

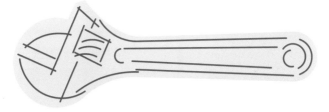

One effective means of creating icons involves forcing a subject to fit within the parameters of a basic shape. Such unnatural boundaries challenge the designer to find solutions that are out-of-the-ordinary. Visually intriguing results are often revealed through this kind of exploration.

Experiment with the restraints imposed by various shapes and forms. Investigate design solutions that strictly obey the confines of a shape, as well as those that make allowances for certain details to break free.

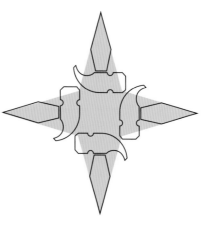

Is there a particular shape that echoes or enforces the overall theme of the icon? Could a relevant graphic element be made to conform to this shape?

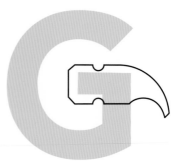

162

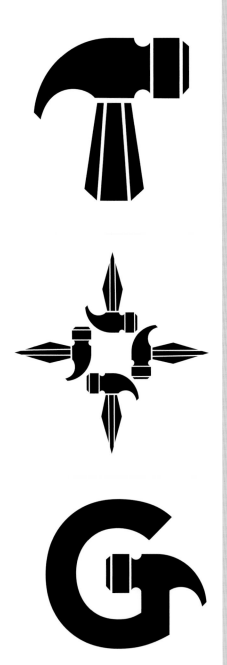

EXERCISE:

Geometric animal icons.

Needed: pen, paper, vector-based graphics software, web access.

In this exercise you will be creating geometric graphic icons based on an African animal of your choosing. Use the web to search for images of your subject. Save images that show your animal from a variety of angles for use as visual reference.

Take a good look at your animal's form and features. What are the visual essentials that sperate this creature from all others? Concentrate on these aspects of your subject as you push, squeeze, simplify, morph and alter its form to conform to the confines of a *circle*, *square* and *triangle*.

You may use all or part of your chosen animal for this activity. Avoid realism; go for the abstract! See how far you can take the simplification process while maintaining your subject's identity.

Begin this exercise with a number of quick pen/ pencil thumbnail sketches before moving to the computer for the finishing stages of production.

You will be able to use one of your designs for the exercise on page 169.

There are an infinite number of ways to visually describe any object or idea.

Q: How does a designer decide which style of presentation and rendering are *right* for a particular icon or image?

A: It's up to the designer, over time and through observation and study, to develop a sense for what look is appropriate for a specific project and what will best appeal to its target audience. For the vast majority of us, there is no shortcut for developing this kind of intuition: start now if you haven't already. Observe, evaluate, take notes, sketch, render, create.

Many designers are themselves capable illustrators and are able to produce icons and images in a number of convincing styles. Other designers stick strictly to design and rely on hired hands to do their illustrative work. In either case, the ability to bring graphic icons from concept to reality through whatever means appropriate is a potent skill for a designer to develop and maintain.

Intuition must be balanced with practicality if a designer is to create icons that are useable in the real world. Will the final product be featured in color *and* black-and-white applications? If so, will it adapt well to both? Does the icon include fine details that might be endangered (as in the sample on the following spread) when the logo is reduced to smaller sizes? Is the design meant for display on the web? If so, will it look good on-screen at various sizes and resolutions?

Strive for visual versatility when it comes to the creation of icons that are meant for broad use and varied media. This will not only make your client happy, it will also make your life easier when it comes to adding the logo or graphic element to actual layouts.

164

ALEXANDRO
WOODWORKING CENTER

The linework used to illustrate a particular image may look good at larger sizes, but will it be reduced to oblivion when the image is shrunk? Will a printing press be able to handle the linework once it has been taken down to a size that is appropriate for a business card or small advertisement?

Pay attention to the spaces between lines as well (as in the upper handle of this chisel). If they are overly narrow, they may clog when the image is reduced. Designers will sometimes create size-specific versions of an icon that are targeted toward small, medium and large uses.

Even after reaching the point where you have nailed down an icon's rendering and relation to typographic elements, subtle variations in its presentation should still be investigated.

Experiment with color and border options before deciding on the final presentation of a logo.

Software makes this kind of last-step exploration fast and relatively painless—there's no excuse to skimp when it comes to the search for the most effective presentation for a logo or image.

ICONS

COMPONENTS

Right: endgame explorations. Even after color scheme, rendering style and compositional arrangement have been finalized, there is still room to investigate options before declaring a logo finished.

Exploring options.

Needed: A shape-oriented animal image from the previous exercise, graphics software.

When you are working on a logo and reach the point where you have a design that feels finished, don't stop exploring quite yet!

Now is the time to put your icon or logo through a few more creative paces before declaring it ready for presentation.

Add a word or two to one of your animal icons for a zoological exhibit. (The samples on page 69 offer several compositional ideas.)

Now, use the computer to explore color-assignment variations.

If you like, export your logo ideas to an image-altering program such as Photoshop for further experimentation with image-based effects. Investigate the effects of drop-shadows, dimension, texture and filters.

Come up with at least a half-dozen aesthetically valid variations of your original logo design. From these, which two or three would you choose for client presentation?

Supporting Elements

Linework, border or backdrop: There is little glory in being a supporting element.

Most often, a successful element of this kind is one that almost escapes notice—enforcing the message and theme of a piece without calling attention to itself.

As designers, we can honor these humble aiding elements by giving them the recognition they deserve and treating them as the potentially powerful building, binding and theme-setting agents that they are.

And while the casual observer might miss the subtleties of a supporting background or bordering element (as perhaps they should if these elements are functioning properly), designers ought to keep a sharp eye out for examples of their use—both successful and otherwise. Save printed samples and bookmark useful web pages for reference and inspiration.

Another good reason to pay attention to supporting elements in the media around us is that they are as subject to the whims of trend as any other kind of graphic element. The savvy designer is ever-attuned to the changing fashions of line weights, border treatments, corner conventions (round vs. square, etc.) and color schemes within backdrops.

> **This chapter focuses on linework, borders and backdrops and their association with other graphic elements.**

SUPPORTING ELEMENTS

COMPONENTS

Hairline

.5 Point

1 Point

2 Point

4 Point

8 Point

Linework can be
used as a BORDER.

Line WEIGHTS are
measured in POINTS (left).

Single line

Double line

Double line, varied weights

Multiple line, varied weights

Tapered

Pattern

Dotted

Dashed

Shaped

Hand drawn

Random

Image

Decorative

Ornate

Linework can be used as a DIVIDER to separate content areas from one another.

LINEWORK usually refers to borders and dividers made of single or multiple lines. Sometimes, "linework" refers to just about any linear element that that functions in this way (samples at left).

Linework is often used as a means of separating and organizing the elements and information in a layout. Linework can also be used to add thematic and stylistic notes to a design.

Linework should only be added where and when it is needed and should not call an undue amount of attention to itself.

172

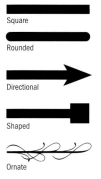

Square

Rounded

Directional

Shaped

Ornate

Lines that are not part of closed formations must come to an END. The ends of lines could be square and precise; rounded to soften the overall feel of a design; tipped with arrowheads; capped with a circle, square or other shape; or decorated for flourish.

BORDER NOTES:

When a border is needed, select a style that complements the look and feel of the overall design.

Avoid borders that compete with or overwhelm their content.

Corners—squared-off or otherwise—are key components in defining the look, feel and function of a border.

Consider printing a border in color or using a tint of an available spot color.

Consider alternatives—see the next four pages for ideas.

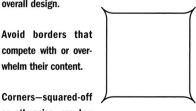

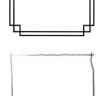

Only the linework varies between these business card designs. In spite of their similarities, the overall appearance of each card is notably different due to the style of linework that has been applied to it. Explore such options, even when a layout is nearly complete. A subtle change in linework may be just the sort of upgrade that will set a particular design apart from the crowd.

A single weight and style of linework can be used throughout a design.

Two or more weights can be combined as long as the differences between them are obvious.

How about dotted or dashed lines? Here, the dotted lines contrast nicely with the solid outer line.

Consider using lines that are not black.

Leaving gaps between lines is a way of subtly departing from the status quo.

How about reversing the linework out of a tinted or solid backdrop?

Linework can be physically embossed, or given a dimensional *appearance* through pseudo 3-D effects.

Would hand-drawn linework suit the project?

Don't be tentative: Avoid combining line weights that do not have clear differences between them.

There are endless ways to use borders to enclose the content of a design.

Borders can be made of lines, graphic elements, ornate designs, words, images, abstract forms and more.

A border should visually and thematically agree with elements it surrounds, while refraining from calling too much attention to itself.

When the *content* of a piece has no obvious stylistic personality, take up the slack by offering thematic clues through the border itself (as in the case of an ornate border being used to enclose the plain text of an announcement).

Remember to take the *space* between a border and its content into consideration. Leave enough space to clearly separate the content from its border, and sometimes, leave even more.

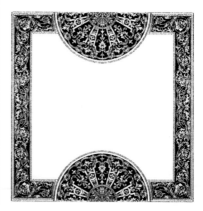

Linework and trend.

Needed: magazines, scissors.

This is a different sort of exercise than those that have come before. This is an observe-and-collect exercise.

Linework is all too easy to overlook. This is partly because linework is rarely supposed to attract attention—rather, its role is usually to help organize and add notes of style to a design.

Look through contemporary magazines and take note of the kinds of linework that seem to prevail these days. Note thicknesses, colors, styles and corner treatments. Clip examples and make a file that can be referenced the next time you are trying to come up with linework ideas for a layout.

Designers who don't keep up with current trends in linework run the risk of using conventions that have fallen from favor with the in-crowd.

177

A backdrop, like a border, is a visual device used to contain and direct attention to a piece's content and message.

A backdrop might be a simple panel of color with text either reversed from it or overprinted on it.

A pattern, design, photograph or illustration might be used as a backdrop.

Naturally, you should avoid using a backdrop that competes, visually or thematically, with the content that overlays it.

Backdrops can be used as "visual glue" to hold together disjointed elements of a design. (See pages 182-183.)

Above: avoid using a backdrop that fights
for attention with the featured content.

Ensuring legibility: headline
over busy backdrop.

Needed: patterns created
for the exercise on page
148 (or gathered from
other digital sources),
graphics software.

Open a tabloid-size
document and draw six
3" x 5" rectangles on the
page. Fill each with a
different pattern.

Now, create a text layer within your document and add
a word over each rectangle
that is thematically connected with its underlying pattern. Choose typefaces that
connect well with each pattern's theme. Set each word
in black at a large size.

Which backgrounds work
well with the overprinting
type? Which backgrounds
interfere with the text's readability? Does reversing the
type, increasing its size,
outlining or adding a drop
shadow help with readability in some cases? Can
certain backdrops be lightened, darkened or otherwise
altered to improve their
association with the
overlying typography?

Get a feel for what works
and what doesn't when it
comes to layering headlines
or other large text elements
over a busy background. To
finish this exercise, make
adjustments to either the
type or backdrop to achieve
a legible result in each of
your six case-studies.

179

Photographic, patterned and illustrated backdrops present the designer with challenges when it comes to placing text or other graphic content on top.

With lighter images, simply printing the text in black or a dark color may be enough to ensure readability. Similarly, when a darker background image is used, white or light-colored text may stand out adequately. A backdrop that is consistently mid-valued might accommodate either dark or light text.

When the content of a backdrop is visually active, additional measures may be needed to give the viewer's eye a chance to find and read the type. Larger, bolder fonts may do the trick—experiment with black, white and colored text to see which (if any) stands out properly. Keep in mind that reversing small or fine text from a dark or busy background can possibly present the printer with difficulties.

If a backdrop is particularly contentious, the text might need to be placed within a black, white or colored block that interrupts the background image. If this feels too abrupt, a translucent panel could be created over the image onto which text could be placed (see the next spread for a larger example of this strategy).

Additionally, most graphics software offers a host of options that can help with text readability when it comes to standing out against difficult backgrounds (halo effects, drop shadows, outline options and more).

At right are several examples of text-over-backdrop combinations. In some, the text is more readable than in others. When it comes to legibility, always weigh the tolerances of your audience: what will they accept? What will they find too busy or difficult to read? Take note of good and bad examples of text/image combinations when you come across them: learn from the successes and failures of others.

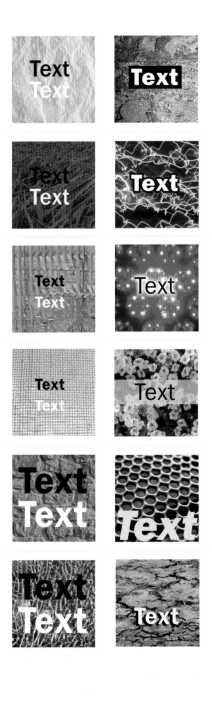

Text "safe areas."

Needed: An image-editing program such as Photoshop, web access.

You'll need a visually busy, colorful image for this exercise (the busier the better). Import one from your own collection or download a sample from the web.

In Photoshop, fill a letter-size document with your image and use guidelines to define a 3" square in the center. Next, fill the square with 9pt. black text (leaving a 1/4" margin around the type). If your backdrop is appropriately distracting, the type should be virtually unreadable at this stage of the exercise.

Now, explore ways of creating a "safe area" for the text that insures the type's readability. Try filling the 3" square with one or more light hues that tie in with colors found in the background image. See what happens when the square is filled with a semi-opaque white or colored panel. Experiment with the application of special effects within the square. See whether or not the addition of a border around the text-safe area helps segregate the type from its busy backdrop.

Save your best legibility-enhancing solutions for future reference.

181

This text would be very difficult to read if it were printed directly over the image in the background.

Here, a translucent panel has been created (using layer and transparency controls in Photoshop) that allows a light tint of the background image to show through while restraining its detail and values enough that text can be safely overprinted.

Problem solved.

There are many ways to handle the readability challenges presented by busy backdrops—especially with the tools available through image-altering software. Four strategies for providing a safe visual environment for text are featured at right.

Abcde fg hij klmno pqr stuvw xyza bc defg hi jklmn op qrs tuvwx. yzab cde fghi jklmn opq rstuv wxy zab cde fghi jklmn opq rstuv wxy zabcde fg hi jklm n. op qrs tuvwx yzab.

Cdefg hi jkl fg hij klmno pqr stuvw xyza bc defg hi jklmn op qrs tuvwx yzab cde fghi jklmn opq rstuv wxy zabcde fg hij klmno pqr stuvw xyza

Bc defg hi jklmn op qrs tuvwx yz ab cde fghi jklmn opq rstuv wxy z ab cde fghi jkl mn opq rstuv wxy zabcdefg hij klmno pqr stuvw xyza bc defg hi jklmn op qrs tuvw xyza bcdefg hi jkl fg hij klmno pqr stuvw xyza bc defg hi jklmn op qrs tuvwx yzab cde fghi

Jklmn opq rstuv wxy zabcde fg hij klmno pqr stuvw xyza bc defg hi jklmn op qrs tuvwx yz ab cde fghi jklmn opq rstuv wxy z ab cde fghi jkl mn opq.

156

Above, the backdrop has been lightened to provide a safe backing for text. Below, Photoshop's Gradient Map filter has been applied to reduce contrast while amping color. The lack of contrast between hues allows the bold type to print with reasonable legibility.

Above, the soft edge of the all-white text panel allows for a smooth transition into the background image. Below, gradations are another way to create a non-jarring transition between a busy background image and a workable text area.

Abcde fg hij klmno pqr stuvw xyza bc defg hi jklmn op qrs tuvwx yzab cde fghi jklmn opq rstuv wxy zab cde fghi jklmn opq rstuv wxy zabcde fg hi jklm n op qrs tuvwx yzab.

Cdefg hi jkl fg hij klmno pqr stuvw xyza bc defg hi jklmn op qrs tuvwx yzab cde fghi jklmn opq rstuv wxy zabcde fg hij klmno pqr stuvw xyza

Bc defg hi jklmn op qrs tuvwx yz ab cde fghi jklmn opq rstuv wxy z ab cde fghi jkl mn opq rstuv wxy zabcdefg hij klmno pqr stuvw xyza bc defg hi jklmn op qrs tuvw xyza bcdefg hi jkl fg hij klmno pqr stuvw xyza bc defg hi jklmn op qrs tuvwx yzab cde fghi

Jklmn opq rstuv wxy zabcde fg hij klmno pqr stuvw xyza bc defg hi jklmn op qrs tuvwx yz ab cde fghi jklmn opq rstuv wxy z ab cde fghi jkl mn opq.

156

Abcde fg hij klmno pqr stuvw xyza bc defg hi jklmn op qrs tuvwx yzab cde fghi jklmn opq rstuv wxy zab cde fghi jklmn opq rstuv wxy zabcde fg hi jklm n op qrs tuvwx yzab.

Cdefg hi jkl fg hij klmno pqr stuvw xyza bc defg hi jklmn op qrs tuvwx yzab cde fghi jklmn opq rstuv wxy zabcde fg hij klmno pqr stuvw xyza

Bc defg hi jklmn op qrs tuvwx yz ab cde fghi jklmn opq rstuv wxy z ab cde fghi jkl mn opq rstuv wxy zabcdefg hij klmno pqr stuvw xyza bc defg hi jklmn op qrs tuvw xyza bcdefg hi jkl fg hij klmno pqr stuvw xyza bc defg hi jklmn op qrs tuvwx yzab cde fghi

Jklmn opq rstuv wxy zabcde fg hij klmno pqr stuvw xyza bc defg hi jklmn op qrs tuvwx yz ab cde fghi jklmn opq rstuv wxy z ab cde fghi jkl mn opq.

The layout at right, first featured in the chapter on compositional grouping (pages 40-49), has been designed to convey a feeling of disconnect and discord. Still, it needs to hold together from a compositional standpoint if it is to succeed aesthetically.

Though subtly presented, the textured backdrop (with its integrated starburst) is critical to the visual integrity of the layout. These supporting elements not only enhance the thematic energy of the design, they serve as the

visual glue

needed to bind scattered elements.

Right, top: By visually linking itself to each element in the design, the textured backdrop also provides a virtual bridge between the elements themselves. Additionally, the starburst in the background helps define a region of focus within the composition.

The poster's sans-backdrop cousin (right, bottom) feels unfinished, scattered.

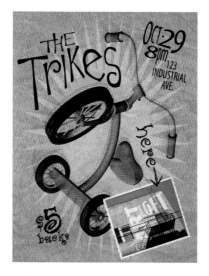

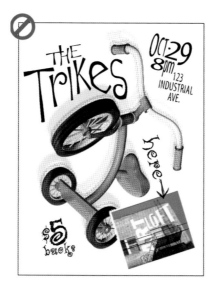

comme

clip art

Clip art: those ready-to-use, often simplistic illustrations of things like businesspeople shaking hands, stacks of wiggling dollar bills, roller-bladers wearing headphones, talking appliances, etc. Do you use them?

ntary:

I don't, and neither do most of the designers I admire and look to for inspiration. And illustrators, well, I think that most illustrators view clip art in the same way that a French chef might view french fries.

Here's the thing: by deciding at an early point in my design career never to use off-the-shelf, pre-fab illustrations, I've been forced to develop certain skills of rendering, photography and, above all, resourcefulness (all skills that might have never germinated if I'd reached for a catalog or visited a clip-art website whenever I needed an image for a layout).

When a project calls for an illustration that lies outside my ability to produce,

I seek a freelancer who can handle it (and, if necessary, engage in some budget-related diplomacy with the client if extra dollars are needed to cover the expense).

As far as stock *photos* go, I do use them from time to time. When, for instance, I need a picture of something that I cannot easily get through a freelance photographer or through the lens of my own camera—a picture of the earth taken from outer space, for example—I use a stock photo.

In summary: I produce the images that I can and hire professionals to do what I can't, but when it comes to clip art, I draw the line (so to speak).

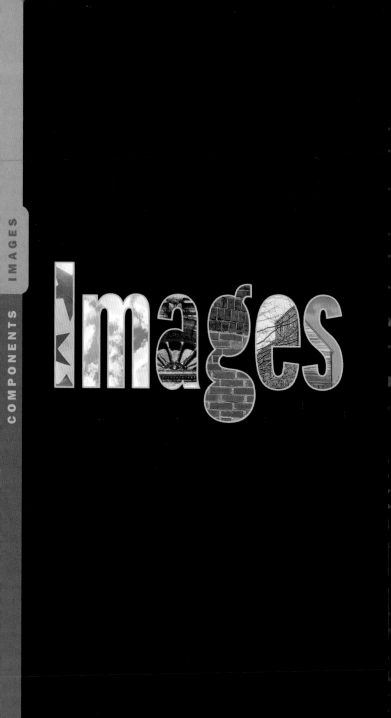

It is said that a picture is worth a thousand words. And whether you believe that or not (writers and typographers being among those who might disagree), it's clear that photographs and illustrations are able to draw attention and establish powerful connections with viewers.

Every viewer of a photo or illustration sees that image differently. An image that is likely to catch and hold a particular viewer's attention is one that possesses at least one of the following qualities: *content that is informative or relevant; content that is intriguing or worthy of further investigation; content that is aesthetically or emotionally appealing.*

Given one or more of these qualities, there is yet another critical consideration to take into account regarding the ultimate success or failure of an image in reaching its audience: *presentation.*

Some illustrators and photographers act as designers when it comes to creating layouts around their images. Some designers produce the illustrations or photos that are used in their own layouts. Whatever the case, the final presentation of an image rests in the hands of whoever is in charge of creating the layout in which it will be featured. And, it's up to this person to decide where and how the image will be placed, if it will be bordered (and in what way), how large it will be in relation to other compositional elements and whether croppings or adjustments need to be made for optimal presentation.

This chapter focuses mainly on the incorporation of images into layouts, with a few notes on their creation as well.

Consider your options

when it comes to the presentation of an illustration, graphic image or photograph.

Take the qualities of the image itself into account. Is it worthy, thematically and aesthetically, of being the layout's centerpiece, or should it provide support for other, more relevant or powerful elements?

How large should the image be relative to the over-all size of the piece? How large should it be relative to the other elements in the design? (Refer to the "Emphasis" chapter beginning on page 62 for more information on visual relationships such as these.)

Should the image be centered within the layout? Should it be placed off-center, along an edge or inte-grated into an arrangement with other elements? Should it span the entire dimension of the piece—top-to-bottom and side-to-side?

Should the image be cropped or modified in any way to strengthen its visual impact? (Both topics are dis-cussed later in this chapter.)

Opposite page: Use the sketchpad and computer to explore a variety of potential presentations for an image before settling on a winner. Is the image essential to the deliv-ery of the theme or message of the piece? If so, should it visually dominate the composition? If not, should it be given a *supporting* role in relation to a headline, text block, logo or other image?

190

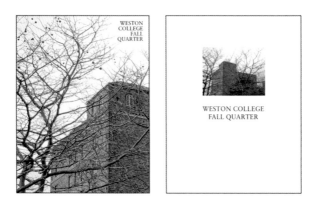

Rarely is a photo ready to go as soon as it leaves the camera.

Depending on what the designer has in mind, the original photo, above, could be cropped in a number of ways.

Along with modifications to an image's color and the application of other digital touch-ups, most photos need to be cropped for optimal presentation.

Crop to eliminate the unnecessary. Crop to improve compositional considerations such as the relative positioning of focal points, spacing and balance. Crop to alter the proportions of an image when it needs to fit into a specific area of a layout. Crop delicately or aggressively.

An image's original quality and resolution should always be taken into account when cropping and enlarging portions from within it.

(A) This cropping eliminates unnecessary and potentially unsightly elements from the lower portion of the photo.

(B) Aggressive cropping can result in an image with an appealing composition and message of its own.

(C) Be on the lookout for details within a photo that could be used for messages other than what was originally intended.

(D) An unusual cropping plus a desaturation of the photo's hues results in an image far removed from the original. (See pages 198-199 for more special-treatment ideas.)

A.

B.

C.

D.

EXERCISE:

Re-composition through image cropping.

Needed: image editing software, digital images.

Select six digital images with varied content: some busy, some plain; some with an obvious center of attention, others without.

Use software to explore variations of each image's original cropping. Be mindful of the principles surrounding eye-pleasing distance relationships (pages 14-37).

Are there tiny or large adjustments that can be made that have a significant impact on the image's aesthetic presentation? What happens when you move your image's center-of-attention to different positions through cropping?

Explore "radical" croppings that drastically alter an images composition and presentation of content. Investigate croppings that result in extreme horizontal and vertical dimensions.

Mentally catalog the discoveries you make during this exercise. Teach yourself to look for image-enhancing croppings whenever you work with photos or illustrations.

Images need not always reside within a box.

A designer can give an image an extra measure of individuality by cropping it in an unusual or unconventional way. Treatments such as these can be used to establish an informal, lively theme for a piece or simply as a creative means of eliminating unwanted details or unattractive areas from a photo.

(A) Images can be contained within relevant typographic elements, shapes or forms.

(B, C) Images can be cropped within geometric or freeform shapes and made to appear as dimensional elements within a design.

(D) A portion of a photo or illustration that has been removed from its background, and is then featured directly against the page, is known as a "knock-out" image. Knock-outs can be performed with image-altering software such as Photoshop. It takes a measure of practice and skill to properly perform this kind of digital feat—especially when working with images that are rich in detail and poor in contrast.

ARCHITECTURAL

A.

B.

C.

D.

There's nothing wrong with presenting a photograph or illustration without a border. Still, there are times when an edge treatment of some kind can be used to enforce or change the context or mood of an image. A blurred edge, for instance, could be applied to the photos within an otherwise highly structured layout to lend a softer, more relaxed note to the overall composition.

Edge treatments can be used to reflect and enforce the mood of an image—moods ranging from passive to frenetic, from ornate to industrial.

Linework: Thick, thin, black, white or colored lines might be used to border an image. Special treatments such as ornamentation or the incorporation of graphic elements around an image might also be considered. Would a blurred, damaged or pseudo-dimensional edge enhance the image's presentation?

Naturally, an edge treatment should not draw attention away from the image it has been applied to unless the border itself is a primary carrier of the piece's message.

Four different examples of edge treatments are featured on this spread. Unless contrast is being sought, choose a border that visually connects with the rest of the layout as well as the look and feel of the image itself.

EXERCISE:

Border variations.

Needed: image-altering or vector-based software.

Select an interesting image from your own digital resources or download a sample from a stock-image website. Crop the image into a square format and arrange six copies on a letter-size document.

Now, explore border options for the images. Come up with solutions that each echo the image's content and concept through color(s), structure and theme.

In addition to the ideas shown at left, consider creating a border by using a pattern, texture, ornament or even slices from other images. Investigate border treatments that use typographic elements.

Experiment with borders that are both subtle and bold, thin and thick, colored and colorless. And remember: a border's role is (almost always) to enhance the image it surrounds—avoid adding a border that calls too much attention to itself.

A digital makeover can give new life to even the most mundane photo.

Adobe's widely-used Photoshop program offers a number of filters and adjustment options that can be applied to any sort of illustration, graphic image or photo. The possibilities are endless when this type of software is combined with a computer that can handle its requirements and a designer that has the creativity and know-how to put them both through their paces.

If you are new to Photoshop, a good place to begin learning about image-alteration is through its Adjustment features. For starters, investigate the Hue and Saturation, Levels, and Gradient Map controls. Using these controls alone, a designer can handle everything from subtle fine-tunings of color and contrast, to eye-popping image radicalizations.

A host of special-effect filters are available within Photoshop as well. These can distort, deform, blur, sharpen, add paint strokes, texturize and (much) more. Play, experiment, explore!

Avoid using effects for effect's sake. Aim toward a result that complements the theme and message of the image and the layout.

On the following page are just a few examples of transformations that can be achieved through Photoshop's controls and filters.

198

Gradient Map adjustments re-apply color information to a photograph: a quick route to a completely new look and feel for an image.

Hue and Saturation controls can be used to significantly alter an image's mood.

Photoshop offers a number of artistic makeover options. Here, the Watercolor filter has been applied to achieve a painterly result.

A pop-art feel has been attained through the use of the Color Halftone filter and the addition of a translucent layer of text.

199

Artistic intuition plays a large role when it comes to deciding whether and how multiple styles of illustration should be combined within a layout. Here's a rule of thumb that can work alongside your gut instinct:

Styles between images should be either identical, or noticeably different.

When identical styles are used between images, the look and feel of that style is amplified.

Contrasting styles, as long as they are working toward the same overall message, can co-exist in harmony because neither style seems to be trespassing on the other's thematic turf.

Contrast in style, agreement in theme. In this poster, the painterly image at top contrasts well with the warmly toned photograph below it. This partnership of contrasting styles succeeds since the individual images are both thematically connected to the subtle historic feel of the overall design.

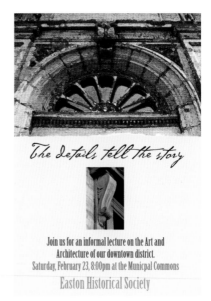

The details tell the story

Join us for an informal lecture on the Art and Architecture of our downtown district. Saturday, February 23, 8:00pm at the Municpal Commons

Easton Historical Society

IMAGES

COMPONENTS

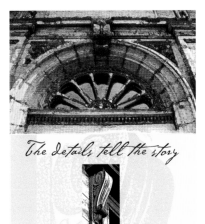

The details tell the story

Join us for an informal lecture on the Art and
Architecture of our downtown district.
Saturday, February 23, 8:00pm at the Municpal Commons

Easton Historical Society

A harmonious trio of contrasting styles. The painting at top clearly stands apart from the high-contrast black-and-white image that sits beneath it. A third, ghosted image of a stippled illustration resides in the background. Again, though each image is clearly different from the others in style and presentation, they all seem to be working toward same thematic message.

The details tell the story

Join us for an informal lecture on the Art and
Architecture of our downtown district.
Saturday, February 23, 8:00pm at the Municpal Commons

Easton Historical Society

A contentious association. The oil painting at top and the colored-pencil illustration below it are both rendered with a similar degree of realism. They seem to be fighting over which way to tell the same story.

Create a savings account of images—one that is always available for reference and use in personal and professional projects.

A suggestion: purchase a camera and get in the habit of taking it with you wherever you go. Keep it in your purse, backpack, pocket or glove-box to make sure it is available whenever you come across an interesting scene or subject. (Note: If you aren't finding yourself coming across scenes or subjects of interest, you're not looking hard enough.) Over time, you will build up a stock of banked images that can be used as featured photos, backdrops, visual textures and reference material for your work.

> *A bonus side-effect of carrying a camera is that it reminds us to look around and helps teach us to really SEE our visual environment.*

Author's note: I prefer digital cameras because they allow me to take a LOT of pictures without fretting about film or processing costs. Plus, the photos I take are ready for use as soon as I can download them into my computer. I keep a small, mid-quality camera with me almost all the time and have a higher-end camera that I take along when I'm specifically going out to shoot photos or when I'm going to be someplace where I suspect that the shooting will be good. I began saving photos in this way about two years ago—and, as of this writing—have a personal image bank of just under 3,500 images. I consider this photo collection to be one of my most powerful and practical assets as a commercial artist/designer.

The photos on the opposite page were all taken during walks around my hometown in N.W. Washington.

comme
rational

The art of rationalization, applied to the rationalization of our art: it's the slow, slinking slide into creative oblivion that cools the original spark that first fired our imagination toward the manifestation of an artistic goal.

It's what happens when we let convenience and happenstance dim and overrule our original creative impulses.

Guard against this stealthy deterioration of ideals. *Always.*

As you work, keep mindful of where you are headed, even if your "destination" at this point is more of a feeling than a clearly pictured outcome. This does not mean that course-corrections en route to a creative objective aren't allowed. On the contrary, they are encouraged—just as long as those course corrections lead to someplace even better, higher, purer, than you were headed before.

Have you ever wondered what you would think of one of your own layouts or illustrations if you were somehow able to leap forward in time and view the final product before you even began? Would you love the final product or would you sense that compromises had been made in the name of speed or con-

ntary:
ization

venience along the way to its completion? Would you be pleasantly surprised by the quality and impact of your own work...or not?

In painting, artistic rationalization sometimes goes like this: the artist wants to paint a flower in the foreground yellow. And look—there just happens to be a puddle of yellow paint sitting on the palette. They ply a bit of the hue onto the tip of the brush and lay it on the canvas. "Perfect," they say to themselves as they finish the flower and move on. But wait, was that *really* the perfect yellow? Did they consider variations, options? Does the hue match what they had origi-nally hoped for when they began the painting and would this be the yellow that would have evolved if the color had been mixed from scratch?

Designers sometimes do similar things when choosing spot colors, typefaces or deciding on the cropping of an image—accepting easily and readily available solutions without compar-ing those choices against the look or feel that they were aiming for when they began the project.

Hold true to your original creative impulses. Avoid the temptations of shortcut and convenience as you journey toward their realization.

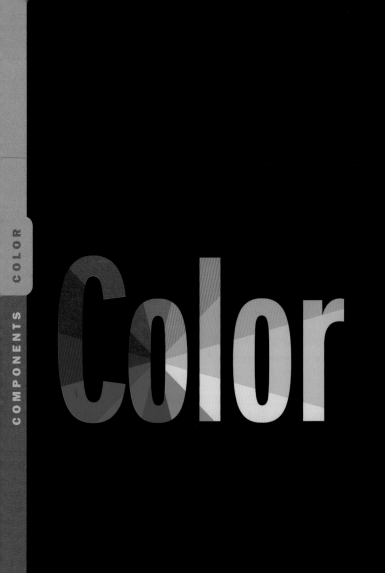

Color

Books can provide us with the terms and definitions that make communication about color possible. They can teach us practical theories surrounding the mixing of hues, the building of harmonious schemes and the technical aspects that a designer must deal with when translating color ideas to print or electronic media.

The rest of our color education happens on a more instinctual level during a lifetime of observation, enjoyment and hands-on practice.

It's the *combination* of our book-learning and the intuition we gain through observational and hands-on experience that endows us with the color-sense that we can then apply to all of our works of art.

Below are two practical suggestions to augment the color-related information and exercises ahead:

1) Turn the computer off once in a while and spend time with watercolors, acrylics, oils or colored pencils. Paint and draw from life and imagination. See what happens when colors are mixed on a palette. Observe the effects that occur when these and other hues are placed next to each other within a painting. Develop palettes and methods of working that convey a variety of moods and effects.

2) Look around! Look at your environment, natural and otherwise: what's really going on out there (near and far) in terms of color? Visit art galleries and take note of what the Great Ones have done—and are doing—with color.

If you are not already fluent in the vocabulary of color, the information in this chapter will help build a foundation. The intellectual study of color helps open our eyes to its subtleties and awaken instincts that can be used in our artistic work and play.

The Color Wheel

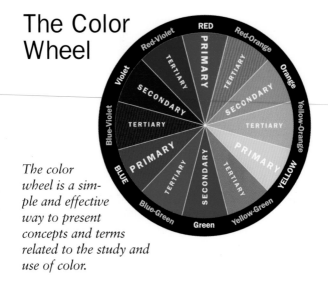

The color wheel is a simple and effective way to present concepts and terms related to the study and use of color.

The **PRIMARY COLORS**—blue, red and yellow—occupy the three foundational spokes of the color wheel. Other colors are created through blends of the primary colors.

Positioned halfway between each of the three primaries are the **SECONDARY COLORS**: orange, green and violet.

TERTIARY colors are created when primary colors are mixed with adjacent secondary colors. Tertiary colors are sometimes referred to as Intermediary colors.

COMPLEMENTARY COLORS are those that are direct opposites on the color wheel. Violet and yellow, for example.

Hue, Saturation and Value

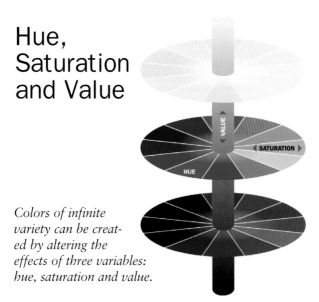

Colors of infinite variety can be created by altering the effects of three variables: hue, saturation and value.

HUE: another name for color—often used in a broader sense to include indistinct shades as well as pure, easily-named colors.

SATURATION: the purity of a hue. A hue that is in its most intense, literal form, is considered *fully* saturated. A hue that is mixed with its complement, black, grey or a neutral tone becomes muted, *less* saturated.

VALUE: a measurement of how dark or light a hue appears relative to black and white. A good way to judge relative value is to deeply squint your eyes when looking at a comparison. Try this with the color wheel on the opposite page—note how the yellow hue becomes obviously much lighter than the blue or violet hues when viewed in this way. Value relationships are crucial when working with color. There is a saying among painters, *"If the value is wrong, the color can't be right."*

COLOR

COMPONENTS

A. The four process colors

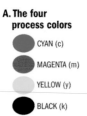

CYAN (c)

MAGENTA (m)

YELLOW (y)

BLACK (k)

As designers working in print media, it is very important to understand how our color choices are translated to ink-on-paper. *Here then, is a crash course (continued through page 212).*

Most color printing is done by using the four process colors of ink (A). Each of these inks is printed from a separate ink tray on the printing press and combined directly on the paper.

B. Tints

CYAN (c)

90%	
80%	
70%	
60%	
50%	
40%	
30%	
20%	
10%	

Process colors can be printed in tints, ranging from 0% to solid (B). Tints are achieved by varying the density of tiny dots used in the printing process (see the enlargement at the bottom of the opposite page).

Process inks are nearly transparent, so when one or more are combined, a new hue results (C). Furthermore, both tints and solids can be combined between one or more process colors (D). An extremely broad range of hues can be achieved in this way using process colors.

C. Combining CMYK solids

100y   100m

100m, 100y

Take a look at the notation at the bottom of (D): this is how a designer specifies colors for process printing (also known as CMYK printing). The number represents the percentage of ink being applied; the letter refers to the ink color itself.

c = cyan; m = magenta; y = yellow; k = black

D. Combining solids and tints

40c   20m   100y

40c, 20m, 100y, 0k

Since the colors you see on your computer monitor will not perfectly

100c, 0m, 40y, 0k

40c, 100m, 0y, 0k

0c, 40m, 100y, 0k

match printed results, it is wise for the designer who works with printed color to keep a process color guide handy (E). These guides provide a reality-check for designers whose digitally created art is destined for print media. Each page of a process color guide shows the *on-paper* results of various mixes between the CMYK inks.

An example: The palette for the illustration at left is shown with the CMYK formulas that the designer used to create it.

Note: While jobs destined for process color printing are designed around CMYK inks, pieces that will be shown in a purely electronic environment (web pages, etc.) are usually designed around the light-based red, green and blue hues of the RGB palette. RGB colors are explained on page 213.

A. Spot Colors

B. Choosing Spot Colors

QUINN'S LICORICE CO

FYI: if this logo were to be printed with spot colors, it would be referred to as a two-color job (black is considered a color on the printing press).

Another common way of printing in color is through the use of spot colors. Whereas CMYK colors are achieved through the mixing of process color inks *as they are applied to paper*, spot colors are custom, *pre-mixed* inks (A).

Think of a quart of spot color ink the same way you would a quart of house paint—its pigment has been selected from a color chart and pre-mixed prior to application.

Spot colors, like process colors, can be printed in tints ranging from 0% to 100% (solid).

And, just as a process color guide is used to select CMYK colors, spot color guides are used to select these hues. Pantone's color guides (B) are used more than any other.

Spot colors are ideal for jobs such as stationery and flyers. Since these pieces often require only two or three colors of ink, it is more cost-efficient to print them using spot colors rather than the four process inks that would be needed to achieve similar results.

As a designer, it is crucial to communicate clearly with printing professionals to determine the best production strategies to apply to any given job.

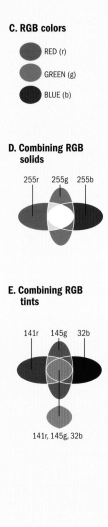

C. RGB colors

RED (r)

GREEN (g)

BLUE (b)

D. Combining RGB solids

255r   255g   255b

E. Combining RGB tints

141r   145g   32b

141r, 145g, 32b

A third language of color that must be understood by the modern designer is the on-screen color vocabulary of RGB (C). All the colors you see on your computer monitor are made up of solids, tints and mixtures of three hues: red, green and blue.

Unlike CMYK colors (which are made of physical, liquid inks), RGB colors are defined through a light-based spectrum of hues. Therefore, when all three solid RGB colors are combined, white results (D). Absence of all three RGB hues means a blank, black monitor.

RGB tints are measured on a scale of 0 to 255. At the high end of each color's scale are its purest hues. The lower the number, the darker the hue (all the way to 0, black). It takes a combination of two or more RGB hues to create lighter tones (E).

Note: Every monitor displays color differently. There is no absolute way to control how your work will appear on another person's computer screen. Digital designs and illustrations should be tested on a variety of platforms before finalization.

And remember that while CMYK-based colors can be represented on a computer monitor, RGB files can NOT be used for printing (since, after all, printing presses print with ink, not light).

213

COLOR

COMPONENTS

Creating harmonious
and effective combi-
nations of color is a
matter of instinct
(honed through prac-
tice and observation),
awareness of trends,
and understanding of
color theory basics.

On this spread, we
focus on five simple
and practical meth-
ods of combining
colors that can be
used as the founda-
tion for building eye-
friendly palettes.

Note: A good way to
begin your search for
a color scheme is to
select a single hue
that seems appropri-
ate for the audience
and message being
addressed. After-
ward, strategies such
as these can be used
to fill out the rest of
the palette.

*Refer to the next
spread for variations
that can be applied
to these (and most
other) schemes.*

Monochromatic
color schemes are
created from a sin-
gle base hue, and
any number of
lighter or darker
tints (value adjust-
ments) of that
hue. Print jobs that
use only one color
of ink are, natural-
ly, limited to this
type of palette.
Monochromatic
schemes can also
be created by using
more and less *satu-
rated* versions of
a base color.

Triads **are created
from any three hues
equally spaced
around the color
wheel. Varied
degrees of satura-
tion can be used
within each of the
three colors to
achieve a more
sophisticated color
scheme. Be sure to
experiment with the
amount that each
color is featured
within a design
or illustration—
regardless of what
type of palette is
being used.**

214

Analogous **palettes** are created when any three adjacent hues are used together. A variation of this type of three-member palette is built by using *every other* color as you move around the wheel from a chosen starting hue.

Complementary **color** schemes are created when any color is paired with its complement. Here, two complementary hues are used along with black. Experiment with introducing black or grayed tones into a complementary scheme. Changing the saturation and/or value of one of the complementary hues might be necessary in order to avoid a vibrating effect between the colors. (See the last sample, page 217.)

Split-Complements are naturally infused with the energy that arises when warm and cool hues are combined. To create a split-complement palette, begin with one hue, and combine it with the two colors on either side of its complement. In this sample, the orange hue has been lightened to avoid a vibrating effect between it and the blue-green—again, see the final sample on page 217.

Whether you are working on a layout or illustration, explore variations in the hue, saturation and value of one or more of the colors within the scheme you are considering. Often, you will be surprised to discover new associations that are more interesting and effective than than before. Here, we take a look at variations that have been applied to each of the illustrations from the previous spread. Use the strategies featured here as the basis for explorations of your own. When you come across effective color combos in print or electronic media, take note! Make an effort to figure out the thinking that the designer used to create that palette.

Monochromatic variation. In this sample, the saturation of two of the blue hues has been heavily muted. Compare this sample with the more saturated version on page 214.

Triad variation. Here, the orange hue has been heavily muted and lightened—to the point where it becomes a neutral brownish tone. The resulting contrast between intense and muted hues lends the image a more progressive feel.

Analogous variation. Each of the hues in this illustration have been heavily muted—all except for the color within the pieces of candy. A single intense hue within a palette of muted tones attracts notice, even if it is used sparingly.

216

Complementary variation. **Compare the look of this illustration with the complementary palette example on the previous page. A slightly quieter effect has been achieved by using a gray tone as a dividing color rather than solid black.**

Complementary variation. **Here, the complementary scheme of before has been given a complete makeover. The colors have been reassigned to smaller roles, the blue muted and lightened and a host of neutral grey values has been incorporated in place of the solid black.**

Split complement variation. **While the red and orange hues from this palette have been left alone, the blue has been expanded into several monochromatic variations. Generally, if a base color works well within a scheme, its monochromatic cousins can also be safely used.**

Here's one that's best to avoid: *complementary colors of identical or similar value.* **The complementary blue and orange hues in this scheme are very close in value. This results in an unpleasant, "vibrating" edge between them.**

COMPONENTS   COLOR

When building a layout around a particular photo or illustration, one of the best ways to create a palette that will complement the image is to borrow colors directly from the image itself.

Many graphics software programs offer tools for taking color samples from within images. Seek hues that both work well together and also relate effectively to the overall theme of the design. Each of the palettes used in the four poster designs featured on this spread were created using colors drawn from the image above.

Lemondrop

218

Lemondrop

EXERCISE:

Color echo.

Needed: image-altering software, a digital image.

Create a word/image composition (such as those seen on this spread) that features blocks of color in its border and/or backdrop. Now, use your software's eye-dropper tool to sample a generous number of colors from within the image. Create a palette off to the side of your design that contains these colors. Next, apply compatible sets of your sampled colors to various elements of your layout. Come up with three different color-schemes for the design. Use this color-echoing strategy the next time you are looking for harmony between image and palette.

Lemondrop

Lemondrop

A designer working within a tight print budget is not bound to lackluster results. Strong design does not need a full palette of colors to convey its message.

A well-chosen color of ink can be flooded over a surface, featured in any number of lighter tints or combined with one or two other inks for cost-effective impact.

Remember to consider paper choices other than white bond for your projects.

Use the ideas presented on this spread as the basis for making the most out of limited printing resources. And again, consult with a print professional to determine how to best prepare your artwork to achieve the effects you desire.

A three-color design for a stationery package. Plenty of inks for a strong presentation within a modest budget.

A two-color design that looks more like three. Here, tints of the orange ink have been used to create a lighter orange hue. Tints can be used to visually expand a limited print budget.

Another two color design, this one taking advantage of the paper in the background to introduce white into the scheme of the logo.

When limited to a single color of ink, you can expand its hue into a monochromatic palette of related tints. Be sure to choose a color that is dark enough to allow for a wide variation of values.

Logo variations.

Needed: an icon created for one of the exercises in the Shape Workshop chapter (pages 124-151), vector-based graphics software.

To begin this exercise, add typography to your icon to create a logo design.

Now, imagine that this logo has been accepted by a client, and that they are asking for four versions of the design to cover all of their media needs:
1) black-on-white;
2) two-color (spot colors);
3) three color (spot colors); and
4) full color (cmyk versions of spot colors).
Remember: black counts as a color when it comes to printing. Also keep in mind that tints of any color may be freely used.

Begin by deciding on a palette for the full color version of your logo. Use Pantone spot colors for your choices and translate to cmyk colors using your software. Next, remove one color and make the necessary adjustments to come up with a three-color version (this time, leave the colors in spot mode). Then, remove another color and readjust the remaining two hues to create the two-color version of your design. Lastly, create a logo that uses only black ink against a white background.

Applying different sets of colors to an image has a tremendous effect on the look and feel of its presentation.

0c	20m	100y	0k
10c	100m	100y	0k
100c	70m	0y	0k
50c	0m	10y	0k

Primary colors lend a feeling of simplicity and directness.

This spread provides an idea of the many directions that can be pursued when looking for effective color combinations.

Software makes experimentation among palettes easy and relatively painless. If you are using the computer to create your illustration or layout, take advantage of its capabilities!

90c	100m	0y	0k
0c	80m	100y	0k
80c	0m	40y	0k
0c	50m	100y	0k

Bright secondary colors can be used to convey action and excitement.

Few areas of design are as subject to trend as color. Look, study, collect samples, explore!

100c	80m	0y	0k
80c	100m	0y	20k
30c	100m	80y	10k
20c	70m	100y	0k

Historically, deep hues of violet, blue, maroon and gold have been used to convey richness, security.

	0c	50m	70y	0k
	0c	70m	70y	10k
	10c	20m	80y	30k
	10c	0m	80y	10k

Unexpected combinations of hues are often sought when a progressive theme is desired.

	30c	60m	80y	30k
	0c	30m	40y	0k
	0c	60m	100y	20k
	0c	5m	40y	0k

Earthtones can be use to give a piece a natural, inviting feel.

	20c	0m	100y	0k
	60c	60m	70y	20k
	30c	30m	50y	30k
	40c	50m	40y	30k

A color can be made to really "pop" when partnered with extremely muted hues.

EXERCISE:

Color trends.

Needed: a few up-to-date, well-designed magazines (buy them, check them out from a library or look through copies at a newsstand).

If you want to keep up with current trends in color, you have to give them your nearly constant attention.

Do this: collect a stack of contemporary magazines and LOOK at the colors and schemes being used.

Also do this: LOOK at what's going on in other forms of current media (movies, fashion, home decor, etc.)—from the avant garde to the corporate. What's going on *right now*?

When you see palettes that appeal to you, try to grasp the thinking behind them. Ask yourself, how are the colors in this scheme related to each other? Do the palettes follow any of the formulas discussed on pages 214-217? Could a palette such as this be useful for any of my current or future projects?

Color trends shift constantly; repeat this exercise often!

223

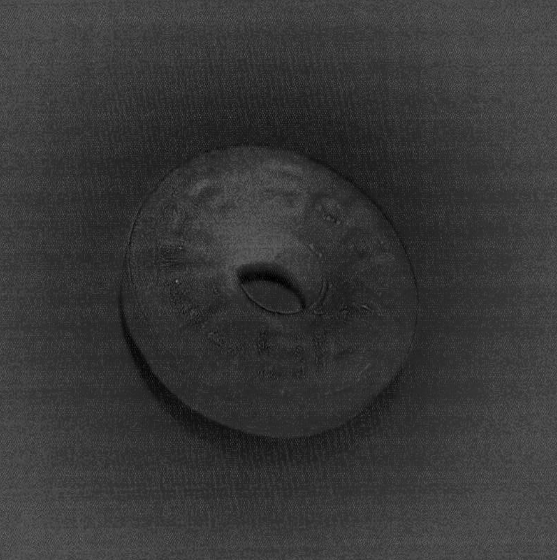

Never underestimate the power of a simple palette.

COMPONENTS COLOR

Stock your creative reservoir with palette ideas and practical color know-how. Clip appealing hues and combinations from magazines and save them for future reference; take out your paints and investigate the effects of mixing pigments on paper. Explore, have fun, become intimately acquainted with the subtleties of color.

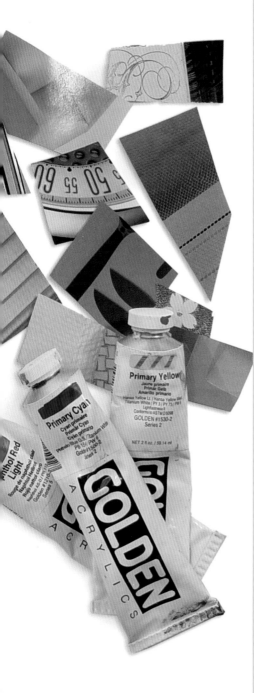

Needed: misc. paints, brushes, paper.

Many designers found their way into the field of commercial art via their love for painting, drawing and other fine arts. Few designers, however, make or take the time to continue working with paints and colored pencils once they enter the consuming world of professional design.

This exercise is really a prompt—an encouragement to rescue dormant art supplies from obscurity and put them to use. And the reason this exercise/prompt is placed within a chapter on color is because there is no better way to learn about color than by mixing pigments on a palette and applying them next to each other on canvas, cardboard or paper.

Consider taking a set of watercolor supplies with you to the park some afternoon and doing some color sketches of your surroundings. How about creating a series of self-portraits or portraits of friends? Or what about hanging some large sheets of paper on a wall someplace where you can try out some crazy abstract explorations?

MUCH is learned about color when we mix it and apply it for ourselves.

Which of these qualities is indispensible to the designer who wishes to survive and thrive in the field of commercial design?

A) Artistic talent
B) A savvy understanding of both design history and trend
C) The ability to gracefully endure criticism
D) All of the above

The answer is C. Without it, a designer simply won't be invited to stick around long enough to nurture the other two (and very important) qualities.

As a commercial designer, your work will be critiqued, and not always by people as smart as you. Can you handle that? If not, can you learn to?

The trick is to not view criticism as a negative; the trick is to keep your ruffled feathers hidden; the trick is to give the critic credit for wanting the same thing you do—a design that effectively conveys the message; the trick is to avoid saying anything that puts the criticizer in a position where they feel that they have to

keep

ntary:

defend their position in order to save face; the trick is to listen to what your conference-room adversary is saying and to consider the possibility that they may be right; the trick is to believe that somehow, some way, a compromise can be found that satisfies the client without sacrificing artistic integrity; the trick lies in being quick to admit when someone else has an idea that's better than yours.

When dealing with clients and critics, stay calm and light. Irritation breeds irritation. Calmness and humor diffuse dissent and help keep the conference room environment amicable.

It's no mere coincidence that most of the great designers that I know, in addition to being highly skilled artists, are problem-solvers, peacemakers, and powerful but gentle persuaders: these are the very qualities that have kept them in the game long enough to become the superstars that they are.

cool

Typography

Typefaces give voice to words.

TYPEFACES GIVE VOICE TO WORDS

Typefaces give voice to words...

The credits begin to roll and the audience waits in eager anticipation for the movie's opening scene. But look, there's a graphic designer in the crowd and she is already enraptured by what she sees! For there, on the screen, are eight-foot-high characters from the Univers family of type; Univers 45 Light and Univers 66 Bold Italic—both from the hand and mind of a typographic giant of the twentieth century, Adrian Frutiger. Ecstacy!

Sound farfetched? Don't believe it? Ask any card-carrying typophile—typography, to many who have studied its varied contours, curves and characters, is a passion that borders on obsession.

Few (if any) forms of artistic expression are as widely seen and as seldom noted as the letterforms of the great typefaces we encounter in our daily lives. A shame, since some of the most aesthetically sensitive artists who have ever lived created these self-contained, sublimely crafted masterpieces. As designers, we have much to gain by taking note of the visual language that the great typographers have used to make language visual.

This is the longest chapter in *Design Basics Index*. It is meant to serve as an introduction to the variety and subtleties of the function and form of type.

Love at first type.

**Opposite:
a lowercase
character from the
HTF Requiem family.
of type. Every detail
is worthy of study,
appreciation
and adoration.**

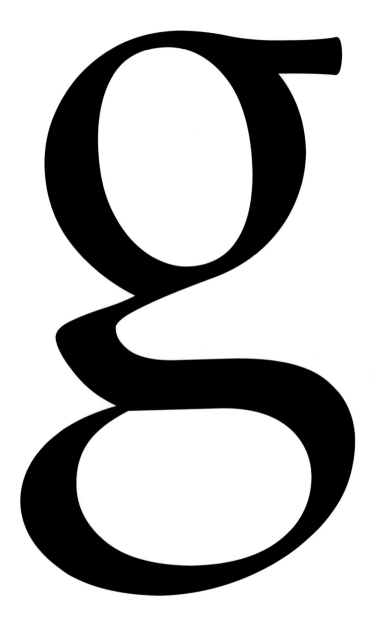

Type:

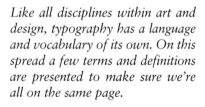

Serif

Sans serif

Like all disciplines within art and design, typography has a language and vocabulary of its own. On this spread a few terms and definitions are presented to make sure we're all on the same page.

A **FONT** is a specific set of typographic characters that are designed to work together. Fonts are also referred to as **TYPEFACES**. The large headline above this column is set in a typeface called Sabon Regular. Individual fonts are often part of **FONT FAMILIES** that contain variations of that font—regular, bold, italic, bold italic and others.

The majority of font families fall into the categories of either **SERIF** or **SANS SERIF** (pages 236-237). A **SERIF** font features horizontal and vertical details that are added to the beginning and end of its characters' major strokes. A **SANS SERIF** typeface does not have serifs—*sans* means "without" in French.

Four other categories of fonts are described on pages 238-239.

a a a a a a a a a a

4pt 6pt 8pt 10pt 12pt 18pt 24pt 36pt 48pt 72pt

24pt 24pt 24pt

a a *a*

CASLON 540 | ITC FRANKLIN GOTHIC BOOK | KUENSTLER SCRIPT MEDIUM

Type sizes are measured in **POINTS**. There are 72 points in an inch. However, be aware: different typefaces of the same point size will not necessarily have characters that are the same height. This anomaly has to do with the way type was once measured in relation to the metal blocks from which it was printed.

cap-height

Xx x-height

baseline

ascender

dp

descender

Often-used typographic terms are illustrated in the middle and bottom illustrations at left.

A typeface's **WEIGHT** describes how heavy it appears. Many font families feature weights ranging from light to heavy to extra-bold.

Typefaces are sometimes **CONDENSED** and sometimes **EXPANDED** beyond "normal" proportions.

Some typefaces are slanted. **ITALIC** typefaces feature characters specifically designed for a slanted presentation. **OBLIQUE** faces are usually made of letters that are simply slanted versions of their regular, non-oblique counterparts.

On this spread and the next, we take a look at six categories into which most fonts fall: Sans Serif, Serif, Script, Monospace, Novelty and Dingbat.

Every category has its place in the designer's creative arsenal. It takes a practiced and observant eye, an awareness of trend and an understanding of one's audience to determine which category of font, and which typeface in particular, best suits a project.

Whenever possible, use the computer to explore font options. Compare words and blocks of text that are set in different typefaces. Which exhibit the best connection to the desired look and feel of the overall layout?

Typography may well be the most fickle and fluid of all design fashions. It is crucial that a designer be aware of current trends in typography. Keep an eye on typographic websites, type catalogs and current publications of all genres.

Sans Serif

Even though the faces in this category may seem similar at first glance, a great range of effects exists among sans serif fonts. Many families of sans serif fonts are offered in a wide variety of weights and widths. (See page 240 for a partial showing of the extensive Franklin Gothic family.)

Design

HELVETICA LIGHT

Design

AVENIR 95 BLACK OBLIQUE

Design

ITC FRANKLIN GOTHIC BOOK ITALIC

Design

HOUSE GOTHIC LIGHT EXTENDED

TYPOGRAPHY

COMPONENTS

Serif fonts date back to the era when people first took chisel to stone. Within the serif category there are many distinctions. (Three sub-categories of serifs are shown at right.) Serif fonts are particularly suited to longer passages of text; their serifs help provide a horizontal line-of-reference for the viewer's eye as it reads through the content.

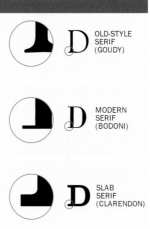

OLD-STYLE SERIF (GOUDY)

MODERN SERIF (BODONI)

SLAB SERIF (CLARENDON)

Design
GOUDY

DESIGN
CHARLEMAGNE

Design
BODONI ANTIQUE

Design
BIRCH

Design
CLARENDON

Design
LUBALIN GRAPH

Design
HTF REQUIEM DISPLAY ITALIC

Design
MONA LISA RECUT

237

Script, Hand-lettered

Script fonts gain their inspiration from hand-lettered forms, both old and new. Some script fonts are calligraphic in nature; others have been created based on the letterforms of handwriting. Be aware that legibility varies greatly among scripts and hand-lettered fonts.

Design

KUENSTLER SCRIPT

Design

FRENCH SCRIPT

Design

P22 CEZANNE

Design

ZAPFINO

Monospace

The characters of most fonts are each a unique width, as are the spaces around them. The character and spacing widths within a *monospaced* font are all identical. Typewriters use a monospaced system for their letterforms. Many modern fonts that are designed for pixel-based, on-screen presentation are also monospaced. These fonts often contain a combination of serif and sans serif characters.

Design

ANDALE MONO

Design

MONACO

Design

LOVE LETTER TYPEWRITER

MAGDA CAMEO

Novelty

Anything goes in this category—from the slightly tweaked to the utterly bizarre. Novelty fonts tend to come and go from the graphics scene like shooting stars—spectacular and short-lived. Still, certain novelty fonts, like certain fashion trends, resurface regularly over time.

Dingbat, Ornament

The keyboard can also be used to place images. Dingbat and ornament fonts are comprised of images, graphic elements and flourishes. Some designers use font-creation software to develop their own ready-to-use sets of images.

ASTIGMA

ZAPF DINGBATS

Design

GYPSY SWITCH

WEBDINGS

Design

HOLLYWEIRD

REQUIEM DISPLAY ORNAMENTS

DESIGN

BUZZER THREE

HOEFLER TEXT ORNAMENTS

ABCDEFGHIJKLMNOPQRSTUVWXYZ
abcdefghijklmnopqrstuvwxyz 1234567890

ABCDEFGHIJKLMNOPQRSTUVWXYZ
abcdefghijklmnopqrstuvwxyz 1234567890

ABCDEFGHIJKLMNOPQRSTUVWXYZ
abcdefghijklmnopqrstuvwxyz 1234567890

ABCDEFGHIJKLMNOPQRSTUVWXYZ
abcdefghijklmnopqrstuvwxyz 1234567890

ABCDEFGHIJKLMNOPQRSTUVWXYZ
abcdefghijklmnopqrstuvwxyz 1234567890

ABCDEFGHIJKLMNOPQRSTUVWXYZ
abcdefghijklmnopqrstuvwxyz 1234567890

ABCDEFGHIJKLMNOPQRSTUVWXYZ
abcdefghijklmnopqrstuvwxyz 1234567890

ABCDEFGHIJKLMNOPQRSTUVWXYZ
abcdefghijklmnopqrstuvwxyz 1234567890

ABCDEFGHIJKLMNOPQRSTUVWXYZ
abcdefghijklmnopqrstuvwxyz 1234567890

ABCDEFGHIJKLMNOPQRSTUVWXYZ
abcdefghijklmnopqrstuvwxyz 1234567890

ABCDEFGHIJKLMNOPQRSTUVWXYZ
abcdefghijklmnopqrstuvwxyz 1234567890

ABCDEFGHIJKLMNOPQRSTUVWXYZ
abcdefghijklmnopqrstuvwxyz 1234567890

ABCDEFGHIJKLMNOPQRSTUVWXYZ
abcdefghijklmnopqrstuvwxyz 1234567890

ABCDEFGHIJKLMNOPQRSTUVWXYZ
abcdefghijklmnopqrstuvwxyz 1234567890

ABCDEFGHIJKLMNOPQRSTUVWXYZ
abcdefghijklmnopqrstuvwxyz 1234567890

ABCDEFGHIJKLMNOPQRSTUVWXYZ
abcdefghijklmnopqrstuvwxyz 1234567890

ABCDEFGHIJKLMNOPQRSTUVWXYZ
abcdefghijklmnopqrstuvwxyz 1234567890

240

Certain font families feature a broad array of weight and width options, making them

versatile and effective choices for a wide range of projects.

A partial showing of the ITC Franklin Gothic family is featured on the opposite page. Weights range from the very light to the extremely bold. Widths vary from extra-condensed to condensed to regular (some font families also include "extended" versions of themselves).

Most large font families carry with them a large price tag. Depending on the kind of work you do, it may be prudent to invest in one or more carefully selected packages such as this to cover your typographic needs.

Legibility, the ease with which a viewer can read a headline or passage of text, is a crucial considera- tion when it comes to choosing and using a typeface.

The designer must remember that their own ability to deci- pher text that is pre- sented in a particular font may not be the same as the ability of others who will be trying to read the same text.

Identify and evaluate the legibility toler- ances of your target- audience. Older and conservative audi- ences are usually less tolerant of diffi- cult-to-read fonts than younger and progressively-minded audiences.

Many factors affect legibility: font choice, size, color, letterspac- ing, case (upper vs. lower) and the back- drop behind the text.

Type that is presented in upper *and* lower case is generally considered the easiest to read.

A *serif* font, upper and lower case, is the pinnacle of legibility—especially for extend- ed passages of text.

All-caps are fine in short bursts (such as a headline or brief caption) but raise readabil- ity issues when used for longer passages.

Too much or too little letterspacing can inter- fere with legibility. The designer must decide what is acceptable for a given purpose.

Novelty fonts do well in conveying certain themes, though sometimes at the expense of legibility.

Always take the eyesight of the target audi- ence into account when choosing a type size. Small text may alienate older readers.

Color also affects legibility. Again, the eye- sight and expectations of the audience are critical factors in determining what's okay.

Extremely condensed typefaces may solve fit issues within a layout, but be aware of the loss of legibility inherent in these faces.

The same pros and cons apply to extremely expanded faces.

Progressively-minded viewers are often more tolerant of legibility issues than more conservative audiences.

...and then there are fonts that are nearly impossible to read—by design.

Typeface legibility

Typeface legibility

TYPEFACE LEGIBILITY

TYPEFACE LEGIBILITY

TYPEFACE LEGIBILITY

Typeface legibility

Typeface legibility

TYPEFACE LEGIBILITY

Typeface legibility

Typeface legibility

Typeface legibility

Typeface legibility

Some fonts were created with text block readability in mind. Other fonts sacrifice a degree of legibility in pursuit of aesthetic or stylistic goals. Note the varied degrees of legibility evident in the text passages on this spread.

Most of the serif text used in this book (including this paragraph) is set in a font named Sabon. Sabon is ideally suited for large blocks of text: its smooth, gracefully tapered serifs help guide the eye through each paragraph, the contrast between its thick and thin strokes is minimal (thus lending an even visual tone to blocks of text set in this font) and it is available in both *italic* and **bold** variations for different levels of emphasis. In general, *oldstyle* serif fonts (see page 237) make good candidates for use in large blocks of text.

Many *modern* serif fonts are also reasonably adept as text fonts and lend paragraphs a sharp, progressive feel. Their hard-edged serifs are less fluid than those of an oldstyle serif font, and thus, are less suitable for high-volume appearances such as in books and text-heavy brochures. This paragraph is set in Bodoni Antique.

Slab **serif fonts, such as Clarendon, are less readable than either of its serif cousins shown above, but are still suitable for blocks of text that are modest in length. Advertisements from days past, as well as some retro ads of today, often feature text using slab serif fonts.**

The added level of detail inherent in italic typefaces tends to be distracting when it comes to large amounts of text—making these faces less appropriate for lengthy passages than their upright relatives. Still, there are times when large blocks of italic text are acceptable, such as when quoted or highlighted text needs to be presented in a way that differentiates it from other, non-italic text.

244

Sans serif fonts, such as the Futura used here, are generally not well suited for large blocks of text. Lacking serifs, these fonts do not provide the eye with the helpful, horizontal guidelines of a serif face. Still, sans serif fonts are perfectly appropriate for headlines, captions and text blocks of shorter duration.

Bold fonts, whether serif or sans, are appropriate for short blocks of emphasized text or captions that need to stand apart from other text. However, used in longer passages, these fonts appear heavy-handed and are not particularly eye-friendly.

SETTING LONGER PASSAGES OF TEXT IN ALL CAPS, SERIF OR SANS, IS NOT A GOOD IDEA. IT CAN BE AS ANNOYING AS LISTENING TO SOMEONE SHOUTING FOR A LONG PERIOD OF TIME—ONLY APPROPRIATE WHEN AN INTENTIONALLY JARRING EFFECT IS DESIRED.

Script fonts are suitable for short blocks of text and traditional uses such as invitations.

The readability of any sort of unusual font must be carefully considered before committing it to text passages. Who is the audience? What will they accept?

Font selection is not the only factor that affects a text-block's legibility. See the following four pages for more variables that are worth taking into account.

White text that has been set against a black background (also known as reversed text) is considerably less readable than black text set against white. There are times, however, when it's okay to reverse text, such as when the look and feel of a design demand an unconventional presentation (and then, only if the target audience seems likely to permit a loss of legibility in favor of this darker look). Sans serif fonts of medium or bold weight are easiest for the printer to handle since they don't contain the fine details of serif or script type that might fill in during printing. Try to keep the length of reversed text to a minimum.

The alignment of type within a text-block plays an important role in determining its readability and relation to other elements in a composition.

The most common methods of alignment are **flush left, flush right, justified and centered.** At right are samples of each of these conventions.

Unless the text size is s m a l l enough, it's difficult to avoid spacing problems when setting justified text in a narrow column.

FLUSH LEFT TEXT

The alignment of this block of text is *flush left*. This means that the left edge of the text is aligned vertically. Sometimes this arrangement is referred to as *flush left, ragged right* (since the right edge of the block is ragged). The aligned left edge of the text helps assure readability by provided the viewer's eye with a consistent and predictable starting point for each new line of text. The ragged right edge lends an informal note to a column of flush left text.

FLUSH RIGHT TEXT

The text in this column is vertically aligned along its right edge. *Flush right* text is not as reader-friendly as flush left text since each new line begins in a different horizontal position. Flush right alignments, therefore, are not well suited for long passages of text. This arrangement can, however, be a useful means of establishing a clean visual association between a *small* block of text and other elements aligned along its right edge.

JUSTIFIED TEXT

Text that is *justified* is vertically aligned along both its left and right margins. Justified text presents itself in a formal, readable manner. Most books and magazines feature text in justified columns. When the computer sets justified text, minute adjustments are made to the letter and word spacing that force each line fill to span the full column width. Sometimes this results in awkwardly large or small letter/word spaces within the columns. In these cases, the designer should be willing to make manual adjustments to create a more even visual flow of text. Columns that are very narrow are not well-suited for justified text since they often require the computer to make extreme letter/word space adjustments in order to force the text to conform to the restrictive columns (example at left, bottom).

CENTERED TEXT

This block of text is vertically centered;
both its left and right edges are allowed to run
ragged. Readability is reduced because of the dual
ragged edges (especially when centered text is used in
wide columns). Thus, it's best to use centered alignment only with columns that relatively narrow and
with shorter blocks of text. Inexperienced designers
often tend to over-favor centered text.

Rule of thumb: Avoid mixing different alignments between headline and text (e.g., a centered headline over flush left or flush right text).

CENTERED HEADLINE

This headline/text combination illustrates an exception to the axiom stated above. It's okay to center a headline over justified text because, technically, the alignment of the justified text could also be considered centered.

TYPOGRAPHY

COMPONENTS

Leading and letterspacing are two more considerations to take into account when it comes to maximizing the legibility of text or aiming toward a specific visual effect.

SABON REGULAR
10/12

NAME OF FONT

FONT SIZE

TOTAL LEADING

Leading is the amount of space between lines of type. Leading, like type, is measured in points. This text is set in Sabon Regular, 10 point, with 12 points used for leading. The extra two points of space between these lines of text help provide distinction between them and improve the overall readability.

SABON REGULAR
10/10

This text is set "solid," meaning that there is no extra leading between lines. Space restrictions and style considerations sometimes require that text be set solid even though it is harder to read than text with extra leading.

FRANKLIN GOTHIC BOOK
8/7

CERTAIN BLOCKS OF TEXT MIGHT BE SET WITH NEGATIVE LEADING TO CREATE A TIGHTLY PACKED EFFECT.

SABON ITALIC
10/20

Widely leaded passages of text lend an airy feel to a page. This is appropriate when a theme of elegance or leisure is desired or as a means of filling a particular area of a layout with type.

Letterspacing refers to the amount of overall space between the letters in a word or passage of text. With justified text such as this, the computer varies the letter and word spacing within each line in order to force the column to align evenly on both sides.

When text is set flush left, the computer assigns the same degree of spacing between each character, regardless of the fullness of each line of text.

Software commands can be used to reduce letterspacing for a tighter-fitting look such as this (at some expense of readability).

Letterspacing can be increased slightly if the designer feels that a more open feel will suit a layout or purpose.

L e t t e r s p a c i n g   c a n   b e   e x a g g e r a t e d   w h e n   a   n o v e l   e f f e c t   i s   d e s i r e d   (a g a i n ,   w i t h   s o m e   s a c r i f i c e   i n   r e a d a b i l i t y   a n d   t y p o g r a p h i c   c o r r e c t n e s s) .

S O M E T I M E S   A   H E A D L I N E
IS LETTERSPACED TO FILL A COLUMN, OR FOR THE SAKE OF EFFECT

When working with headlines or text, practiced designers often take time to work over the computer's default letter and word space offerings. Manual adjustments to these details can have a great effect on the flow, look and legibility of the type within a layout or publication. (See pages 264-265 for more on these kinds of adjustments.) The most important thing to for a designer to keep in mind when using computers to compose text is this: *Don't take its typographic decisions for granted—let your eye tell you what is acceptable and what needs fixing.*

The use of large initial capitals at the beginning of a block of text has long been favored by designers as a means of drawing notice to an area of text within a layout (and away from more highly emphasized elements such as a headline or photo). In this example, the large T has been placed in a clear, indented space that has been carved into the paragraph that follows. Note that its baseline aligns with one of the text baselines within the paragraph.

As opposed to the method shown above, some designers prefer to follow the contours of an initial cap rather than carve out a block for it to sit in. Some letters work better than others for this treatment. Either way, it is important to be consistent within a layout—not to vary conventions such as this unless variation itself is a theme.

Sometimes an initial cap will be placed in such a way that it sits partway in and partway out of a text column. Large initial caps that are displayed in out-of-the-ordinary ways attract attention both through their relative size and their uncommon style of presentation.

Initial caps are sometimes subtle.

When space permits, an initial cap might be allowed to extend above the text block.

Unusual letterforms can be used as initial caps. Consider featuring characters that have been artfully treated, dimensionally rendered or textured. How about a letter that contains an image within its shape? Would an ornate historic letterform fit the project's theme?

In this book, most of the paragraphs do not have indents. Rather, individual paragraphs are distinguished by leaving blank spaces between them.

A more common way to distinguish between paragraphs is to indent their first line. Note that while the subsequent two paragraphs in this sample *have* been indented to illustrate this convention, this particular paragraph does *not* have an indentation at its beginning.

Why is this? Stylistically speaking, it is considered preferable *not* to indent the first in a series of paragraphs (since, technically, the first paragraph needs no distinction between itself and a predecessor).

How far *in* should an *in*dent go? Just far enough to show that a new paragraph has begun and maybe just a little bit further. Follow the lead of experienced designers rather than typing teachers (with all due respect) when it comes to indents and most other typographic considerations: avoid oversized indents. (And *never* double-space after a period.)

Here's something different: an indent that's really an "outdent." Sometimes an unconventional treatment such as this can add subtle visual flair to an otherwise standard layout.

Here's another trick to add to your typographic repertoire: images placed between paragraphs or sentences. These dingbats, small illustrations, flourishes, or simple bullets not only provide separation but can add visual interest to a block of text as well. **One last non-traditional approach to consider: Indicate the start of a new paragraph through a significant change in the font and/or color of the text.**

Sometimes, within the layout for an ad, brochure or other piece of promotional media, a designer will want to make certain words or pieces of text stand out above other

Emphasis

elements. Several different strategies for typopgraphic emphasis are featured throughout this spread. Keep in mind: unless an emphasized element is *meant* to be the center of attention within a composition, do not grant it so much visual strength that it fights for dominance with, say, a headline or featured illustration. (Refer to "Visual Hierarchy," pages 64-65.)

A message can be highlighted by placing it in a layout's outer margins.

Text might break out of a column, be printed in a bright color, or present itself in a bold font for notice. Or, it could do all of these things at once (above, topmost example).

Look at this text!

Text could wrap around a shape or a graphic silhouette that contains a featured message. Again, color, size and position are each important variables to consider with this kind of add-on.

Colored text calls for attention,

as does type that is relatively large.

For the sake of notice, text elements could be tilted, enlarged, colored, doodled-upon or made to appear dimensional, textured or damaged.

stamped for effect.

A designer might use a block of color, an illustration or a photo

Pink.

as a backdrop for a featured type element. (See pages 180-181 for information regarding text and image combinations.)

NOTICE:
A block of note-worthy text could be placed within a simple border to set it apart from other elements.

P.S. TEXT THAT APPEARS HANDWRITTEN IS HARD TO IGNORE.

TYPOGRAPHY

COMPONENTS

Notes on the columns featured on this spread:

A) Text can safely be presented in a single column as long as the column is not so wide that it makes it hard for the eye to find its place at the beginning of each new line.

B, C) Breaking a text block into two or more columns can make things easier on the eye, and at the same time, provide opportunities for the placement of visual elements within the text. When using columns, be sure that the gutter (the space between columns) is adequate to visually keep them apart.

D,E) A three column format is used in these examples. When columns are narrow, a small font-size or a compressed typeface might be needed to avoid excessive hyphenation or extreme letterspacing. If called for, divider lines between columns might be needed to visually separate them.

F) Experiment with ultra-tight, narrow columns when readability is not a critical issue. Here, readability has been sacrificed in favor of a somewhat novel presentation.

(Text from *The Art Spirit*, by Robert Henri, 1928)

A man possessed of an idea, working like fury to hold his grip on it and to fix it on canvas may not stop to see just how he is doing the work; nor may he consider what might be any outsider's opinion of it. He must hold his grip on the meaning he has caught from nature, and he cannot grope for ways of expression.

A man possessed of an idea, working like fury to hold his grip on it and to fix it on canvas may not stop to see just how he is doing the work; nor may he consider what might be any outsider's opinion of it. He must hold his grip on the meaning he has caught from nature, and he cannot grope for ways of expression. His need is immediate. The

A man possessed of an idea, working like fury to hold his grip on it and to fix it on canvas may not stop to see just how he is doing the work; nor may he con-sider what might be any outsider's opinion of it. He must hold his grip on the meaning he has caught from nature, and he cannot grope for ways of expression. His need is

A man possessed of an idea, working like fury to hold his grip on it and to fix it on canvas may not stop to see just how he is doing the work; nor may he consider what might be any outsider's opinion of it. He must hold his grip on the meaning he has caught from nature, and he cannot grope for ways of expression. His need is immediate. The idea is fleeting. He must have technique—but he can now use only what he actually knows. At other times he has studied technique, tried this and that, experimented, and hunted for the right phrase. but now he is not in the hour of research. He is in the hour of expression. The only thing he has on his mind is the idea. As to the elegance of his

A man possessed of an idea, working like fury to hold his grip on it and to fix it on canvas may not stop to see just how he is doing the work; nor may he consider what might be any outsider's opinion of it. He must hold his grip on the meaning he has caught from nature, and he cannot grope for ways of expression. His need is immediate. The idea is fleeting. He must have technique—but he can now use only what he actually knows. At other times he has studied technique, tried this and that, experimented, and hunted for the right phrase. but now he is not in the hour of research. He is in the hour of expression. The only thing he has on his mind is the idea. As to the elegance of his

A man possessed of an idea, working like fury to hold his grip on it and to fix it on canvas may not stop to see just how he is doing the work; nor may he consider what might be any outsider's opinion of it. He must hold his grip on the meaning he has caught from nature, and he cannot grope for ways of expression. His need is immediate. The idea is fleeting. He must have technique—but he can now use only what he actually knows. At other times he has studied technique, tried this and that, experimented, and hunted for the right phrase. but now he is not in the hour of research. He is in the hour of expression. The only thing he has in mind is the idea. As to the elegance of his expression, he cannot think of it. It is the idea, and the idea alone which possesses him, and because it must be expressed,

Subheads

Subheads are like mini-headlines within a block of text. Subheads usually announce beforehand what the content of a specific section of text will contain. This helps the viewer understand and mentally organize content even before they read it. Subheads also provide points-of-reference that enable the reader to locate specific content within the text. The use of subheads grant the designer opportunities to add visual spark to large, and otherwise bland, blocks of text. Samples of several different styles of subheads are presented on this spread.

Over the top

A subhead can be placed over the top of a section of text. Often, the font used for such a subhead will be a bolder version of the one chosen for the text. It might be presented in an italic face, colored, sized one or two points larger than the text, or made into all caps.

IN-LINE SUBHEAD. A subhead can also be placed "in-line" with the text it precedes. Naturally, there needs to be a distinct difference between the subhead's appearance and that of the type that follows.

Extra tall subhead. An in-line subhead can stick out above the text it leads. Here, an italic version of the text font has been used for the subhead.

CONTRASTING FONT

A font that contrasts with the text typeface could be used for subheads. A bold sans serif font might be paired with an old-style, serif font (as seen here). A script or hand-lettered font could also have been used as a subhead in this example to achieve a completely different effect. (See pages 262-263 for more about combining typefaces.)

256

BEHIND Consider unconventional solutions such as placing tinted subheads behind text blocks. Here, a heavy sans serif font has been used for the subhead—its bold weight helps assure the readability of the lightly colored type.

SUBHEAD IN A BOX

Subheads can be contained in graphic elements such as boxes, shapes or images. This subhead has been letterspaced to give it (and the box that encloses it) more visual substance. *The designer must decide how much notice subheads should receive within a given layout and adjust their size, presentation and color characteristics accordingly.*

Subheads in an adjacent column Subheads can be placed in otherwise blank columns alongside the text. These columns could also contain small illustrations or other highlighted content.

Spanning Columns A variation of the above: Here, the subhead breaks into the text-column from outside its boundaries. Interrupting the vertical margins of columns introduces a note of informality to the structure of a design.

LINEWORK

Linework can also be used to separate text from subhead. Use a line weight that does not call too much attention to itself.

When it comes to pairing headlines with text, there are many font and placement options worth considering. *Headlines can be large or small, as long as they are presented in such a way that they attract a proper degree of notice.* Headlines can float above, be placed within, or sit alongside areas of text. *A headline might run vertically up the side of an ad*

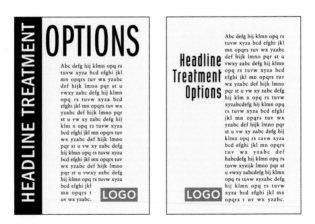

258

or brochure. Its baseline might be horizontal, slanted or curved. *The font used in a headline might match the face used in the text or contrast with it. (See "Combining Fonts" on pages 260-261.)* Whatever you do, be aware of the overall visual hierarchy between the elements of the composition (covered on pages 64-65).

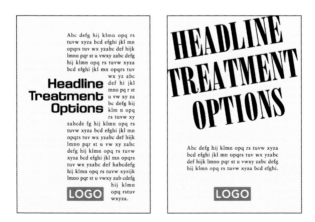

TYPOGRAPHY

COMPONENTS

Don't Let Your Computer Do This To a Head-line

Even the smartest computers make silly design decisions. Be watchful: don't let your computer get away with lousy typographic judgements such as this headline with its unsightly hyphenation and awkwardly short last line.

On a related note, there is something typographically unbecoming about this paragraph. *Do you see it?* It's called an orphan, and, typographically speaking, this term refers to a word that sits all by itself at the very end of a paragraph. Whenever possible, make manual adjustments to previous lines of type in order to either absorb the orphan into the text above, or to give it company in its lonely position at the end of the line.

Avoid setting headlines that seem out of balance.

With its long, heavy first line hanging over a much shorter second line, this header feels precariously balanced, as though about to tip over. When needed, adjust headlines to put them into a more stable, visually balanced arrangement such as the one below.

Avoid setting headlines that seem out of balance.

NEVER, PLEASE.

The gods of legibility, spacing and aesthetics all frown upon all-caps presentations of most script and hand-lettered typefaces.

O U C H

Avoid stacking headline type vertically. It is usually better to turn the type on its side and let it flow up or down. *Still, there are situations, such as when an intentionally funky presentation is desired, when such an arrangement is acceptable.*

Rarely is it a good idea to combine
DIFFERENT SERIF FONTS

THE SAME GOES FOR
SANS SERIF FAMILIES OF TYPE

(More info on font combinations is presented on the next spread.)

And finally, a quote from the legendary type designer, Frederic Goudy:

"Anyone who would letterspace lower case would steal sheep."

A musical duet or trio that is made up of different instruments is able to achieve a quality of sound that could not be replicated if all of the instruments were the same.

Similarly, when fonts from different families are combined in a logo, layout or publication, an interaction occurs that can deepen and enrich the composition.

Combining typefaces is not for the faint of heart: avoid timid decisions! Effective pairings are usually those where discernable and obvious differences exist between the faces. Tepid combinations tend to look like errors or halfhearted attempts at design.

Generally, it is best to limit the number of fonts within a piece to two or less (or perhaps three, if, for instance, a particular font is needed for extreme emphasis). With skill and experience, however, a designer might successfully combine a larger number of fonts to achieve an eclectic look. Refer to designs from the 1800's and early 1900's for examples of extreme multi-font compositions.

Here, a heavy sans serif font has been combined with a light serif typeface. The faces are notably different, as are the sizes in which they appear—a strong degree of contrast that lends richness to this simple combination of words.

In this sample, visual potency has been further amplified by combining fonts with even greater differences between them. A logotype combination that is meant to project a feeling of energy could benefit from a presentation such as this.

Here, a light sans serif font is combined with a light serif font. The association feels weak, timid. To succeed, one of the typefaces would have to be exchanged for something significantly different than the other.

Obvious differences between these faces lend a note of intriguing eccentricity to this pairing. Combos such as this succeed as long as the resulting visual message is appropriate to the theme being advanced.

Remember: The *presentation* of different fonts within a logo or layout can be varied as well.

COMBINING
DIFFERENT FONTS

R **B**

Note the echo between the visual qualities of the negative spaces of these two fonts. Subtle visual connections can be sought if quiet connections between contrasting fonts are desired.

COMBINING
DIFFERENT FONTS

COMBINING
DIFFERENT FONTS

COMBINING
different fonts

COMBINING
DIFFERENT FONTS

TYPOGRAPHY

COMPONENTS

Take advantage of the capabilities of graphics software to make alterations that will enhance the appearance of type that is destined for featured use as a logo or headline. *Below are examples of adjustments that have been made to typeset words in order to improve their visual balance. On the opposite page are finished logos whose type was digitally altered and adjusted to achieve its final appearance.* As a designer, be finicky: take the time to alter and adjust type until it satisfies your aesthetic criteria. Be opportunistic as well—keep your eyes open to cases where graphic intervention can be applied to create intriguing visuals.

COMB

COMB

COMB

Spacing adjustments sometimes need to be made to featured type elements if they are to present themselves optimally. Left, top: The computer's default offering. Note that the M and B are crowded compared to the C and O. At bottom, a more evenly balanced composition of letters.

ATLAS

ATLAS

ATLAS

Sometimes, as when constructing type for a logo, letterforms themselves need to be moved *and* altered to achieve ideal visual relations. Here, graphics software has been used to shorten the horizontal line of the L and thereby tighten its fit with the previously-distant A. The serifs have also been cropped throughout to allow for a tighter fit. Note the seamless connection (ligature) between the A and T.

*There are infinite ways in which graphic and typo-
graphic elements can be combined for the purposes of
a logo, headline or featured image. On this spread are
a few thoughts, examples and axioms to consider.*

The same guidelines that apply to combinations between fonts apply to type and image associations:

combine styles that are either complementary or contrasting; avoid outright conflict.

When is a **COMPLEMENTARY** association the answer?
When should **CONTRAST** be sought?

In general, graphic elements that are visually and thematically **COMPLEMENTARY** amplify whatever visual
theme the two possess. An elegant typeface, for example, could be combined with an elegant graphic element
for—you guessed it—an elegant overall presentation.

CONTRASTING styles can be combined for intriguing,
humorous or sardonic purposes. For example, a
playful feeling of tension might be achieved when an
elegant typeface is paired with a raw and bold
graphic element.

Be mindful of the concepts of effective composition
when working on these kinds of visual connections:
strive for clear visual hierarchy, sensible alignments
and a pleasing sense of balance between elements.

Opposite: Four variations of the logo that was first featured on page
123. In each sample, the visual character of the graphic element either
complements or *contrasts with* the type it accompanies. (Note: A group
of layouts such as this is a good representation of the scope of concepts
that might be offered to a client for a design presentation.)

266

PINPOINT
BENEFIT CONSULTANTS

Pinpoint
BENEFIT CONSULTANTS

PINPOINT
BENEFIT CONSULTANTS

PINPOINT
BENEFIT CONSULTANTS

When new design-
ers first begin to
explore the world of
typography, they
often feel over-
whelmed by the
sheer quantity
of fonts that
are available.

Don't worry. Over
time, this quantity
becomes mentally
divided into neat
and semi-neat cate-
gories—finite divi-
sions into which
typefaces can be
organized and
stored for future use
and appreciation.

In fact, many veter-
an designers tend to
use a core of about
a half-dozen fonts
for the vast majority
of their work—fonts
that, in their eyes,
have no equal in
voice or appeal.

EXERCISE:

Know your faces.

Needed: the type-
faces on your com-
puter, font catalogs or
websites.

When an experienced
designer pulls down a
font menu, they rarely
need to open a par-
ticular font to know
what it's going to look
like—they already
know. This knowledge
helps speed and
enhance their creativ-
ity as they search for
typographic solutions
for a project.

Make the effort need-
ed to familiarize your-
self with your type-
faces. Type the name
of each of your fonts
using the font itself.
Then, explore a few
word associations
using this typeface. If
you have a lot of
fonts, do it piece-
meal—over time. This
activity will help build
your mental card-cat-
alog of fonts and
their uses—a resource
that can and will be
referenced as you
work on projects of
all kinds.

EXERCISE:

Font-watching.

Needed: a selection of
well-designed, contem-
porary magazines.

New and old fonts
are constantly coming
and going from the typo-
graphic in-crowd—and
some stay on the scene
longer than others. Here's
an observational exercise
designed to help you get
up-to-speed with the
world of typography
today.

For this activity, look
through your collection
of magazines with the
purpose of gaining a
clear picture of the
current state-of-the-art
in typography.

Take note of what kinds
of serif and sans serif
fonts seem to be favored
and by whom. Also note
what kinds of script and
novelty fonts are current-
ly popular. If you can,
learn the names of the
specific fonts that you
find appealing (you may
be able to locate these
in font catalogs or on
font-related websites.)

Font-watching is a habit
well-worth cultivating for
all kinds of designers
and it's the only way to
keep up with trends in
this ever-changing area
of our profession.

268

Learn to kern.

Needed: fonts, graphics software.

Experienced designers never take the default settings of the computer for granted when it comes to creating headlines and logos. Usually, the kerning (the amount of space) between certain letters—as well as the overall letterspacing between words—needs to be adjusted to achieve proper overall balance.

Use the words listed below to sharpen your kerning and letterspacing skills. Set each of the words in 72pt. type, in both a serif and sans serif typeface. Once you have the word set on the page, make adjustments to the letterspacing, and, if needed, to the characters them-selves (see pages 264-265 for more informa-tion about these kinds of adjustments) in order to achieve a consistent visual tone throughout the span of the word. You may want to convert the characters to paths in order to more easily alter and adjust them. *You won't be using measuring devices for this exercise—let your eyes and instinct decide what is right.*

CALAMITY

Sanctimonious

AID

ARMADILLO

Psychedelic

Sometimes it helps to print the word on a piece of paper and look at it from across the room during various stages of your transformation(s). Squint your eyes when you look the word and see if certain pairs or groups of letters appear as darker areas than others. Each pair of letters throughout the word should feature the same amount of visual spacing between them.

In addition to striving for consistent spacing among characters, experiment with tight, normal and loose spacing throughout the overall word.

EXERCISE:

Combining fonts and images.

Needed: fonts, graphics software, icons from the exercises on pages 143 and 145.

Visual agreement between fonts and the graphic ele-ments that accompany them is something that designers are constantly aiming for within their lay-outs. The previous page provides some informa-tion on these kinds of associations.

For this activity, come up with a fictitious company name to go with two of the icons created for the exercises on pages 143 and 145. Now, look for a font to use for your company's name that thematically and visually connects with the icon being used. Experiment with font choices and with the placement of the typography in relation to the icon (see pages 68-69 for icon/type examples). Investigate many options before nar-rowing your choices.

Ask: do the curved and straight characteristics of the typeface echo those in the icon? Should they? Or, would contrast between the two suit your theme better? Is there clear visual hierarchy between typography and icon? Which dominates and why?

comme

presentation prep.

Here, at the tail end of our sections on Composition and Components, seems an ideal place to offer a handful of thoughts about the preparation that goes into showing our work, and ourselves, to the client.

The presentation really begins when we first walk into the client's office (or they into ours).

A client's process of evaluation gets underway the moment they see you (not your work, *you*). And yes, while they are surely checking out your physical appearance and outward conduct, what they are really interested in is something a little less tangible.

You see, the client, who has plenty of things to worry about besides how this meeting will go, wants more than anything to be able to look at you and see (for lack of a less flowery way to put it) a glowing, calming aura of unimpeachable confidence radiating outward from your being.

It's true. A designer who is perceived as confident is perceived as having things under control—as someone who is about to make their client's life easier by solving their need for a beautiful logo, ad, brochure, etc. Conversely, a skittish designer can put the client on edge and lead them to wonder if the designer's jitters have anything to do with the layouts that are forthcoming.

Ideally, having basked in the warming phosphorescence of your confident and relaxed manner, the client is them-

ntary:

self calmed. And you, their capable designer, their champion, is off to a great start. *It is much easier to sell ideas to a relaxed client than a worried, defensive, nervous and nitpicking client.*

How is this aura of utter competency acquired? Well, to appear confident, it helps to *be* confident, and to *be* confident, it helps to be as certain as you can that what you are about to present is both ideally conceived and flawlessly executed.

To ensure the best chance of achieving these goals, it is imperative, from the beginning, that you understand the needs of your client, their expectations, tastes (as well as the tastes of their intended audience) and their budget. And since these factors should steer virtually every aspect of the creative work you will be doing for this project, try to gather as much of this info as you can before you begin to create.

One last tip: be sure to preflight your designs thoroughly before presenting them. Take the time to step back and critique every element, placement, color and word within the layouts. Ask yourself if every single creative and conceptual decision that has been made has a good reason to back it up (and remember these reasons—the client may well ask you for them). Fix anything that doesn't stand up to your own blistering review.

Having accomplished all these preparations, lay claim to your well-earned aura of confidence and creative brilliance and let it glow.

Evaluating Components

Put on your Evaluation C.A.P.

Evaluate the components that you create, both by them-selves and within the context of the layouts in which they are appearing. Compare your work with what you see in the larger world of design and if necessary, strive toward improvements that will bring yours in line with— and above—what other designers have done for similar projects. Ask yourself questions about the components you have created based on:

CONNOTATION
ATTRIBUTES
PLACEMENT

In addition to these three criteria, it is important to also judge your work using the C.A.P.s related to Composition and Concept (pages 118-121 and 336-339).

1.
Connotation

Ask:

Does the visual style of this component tie in with the theme it ought to convey? **Is every sub-component within the element working toward the same thematic goal?** Is its theme projected in a way that could be seen as too specific or overly broad? **Could color, proportion, quality-of-finish or font choices within this graphic element be adjusted (if even slightly) to better reflect its message?** Would it be helpful to show the logo or compositional element to others in order to find out if they perceive it the same way as you?

2.

Attributes

Ask:

Are you satisfied with the visual weight, structure, color and presentational style of the logo or graphic element? **Could linework be thickened, made thinner or "roughened up" in order to better establish the element's aesthetic and thematic integrity?** Is this graphic or typographic element associated with a backdrop? **If so, does the element stand out clearly and is it in thematic agreement with the backdrop?** Have color options for each component been explored? **Will the color scheme of each element fit in well with the scheme of the larger layout in which they are placed?** Is the element intended for broad use (i.e., a logo)? If so, has it been designed in such a way that it can be presented in a wide variety of sizes and displayed in various sorts of media? Is the typography appropriately legible? **Is the text large enough for the intended audience to easily read?** Does the look and feel of the type connect with the overall message? **Is it time to look for new fonts?**

274

3.

Placement

Ask:

Should this component be given a starring or a supporting role within the layout? **Should it call attention to itself or go virtually unnoticed?** Something in-between? **What sort of placement should this graphic element be given within the composition?** Should its edges align with other elements within the layout? **If so, will it conform to the same alignment conventions that apply to other elements in the composition (flush left, flush right, centered, etc.)?** Should this element be visually grouped with others for conceptual and aesthetic gains? **Once placed within a layout, should the element be further cropped, rotated, moved, sized or altered in any way?**

Concept is
King.

Concept is
also Queen,
Court Jester, Czar,
Prime Minister,
Head Honcho and
the Big Kahuna.

Concept is
abstract, intangible
and untouchable—and
yet, without its binding
influence, the elements
of a design fall from
the page and land in
the gutter.

Concept is
notion; idea; direction;
look-and-feel; the point
behind the point.

Concept is
car; driver; map.

Concept is
delivered through
connotation, theme,
words, typography,
images, decoration,
composition and style.

If concept were visible,
what would it look like?

This.

→

Concept carries weight.

Concept simply is.

Concept, when it is effectively applied,
demands and hooks the viewer's attention.

Being an abstract, how is concept delivered to the viewer's eyes and mind?

Concept is delivered through the prose of conveyance.

With visual media, conveyance is the delivery of meaning or mood from the observed to the observer.

Clothing and automobiles convey. Architecture conveys. Couches, chairs and tables convey. Salt shakers convey. Your designs convey through words, typography, images, decoration, composition and style.

The conveyances that reach us through what we see are capable of nothing less than shaping the way we perceive, feel about, view and react to our entire sphere of reality.

Consider the Sistine Chapel, the Statue of Liberty, a 1968 Honda Black Bomber motorcycle, the color red.

Conveyance is relative. It is important to understand your audience in order to know how to connect with them through conveyance.

Applying conveyance is largely a matter of instinct—an instinct developed through living, looking, thinking, feeling and doing.

> **The following spreads provide several examples of conveyance at work. The world around you provides countless others. Take a look.**

Both the content of a layout and the style in which the content is presented carry meaning to the viewer. This is conveyance in action.

Conveyance can be uplifting, ominous, passive, aggressive, energetic, erotic, restful or a thousand other adjectives.

Images, layout conventions, typography, and words themselves all convey...*something*. The designer must rely on instinct and experience to decide if that *something* is the the right something for the message and audience being addressed.

Conveyance is everywhere. Conveyances are striking you right now, as you read these words presented in this italic typeface, and even as your peripheral vision notes the cordial handwriting above this text and the organic movement of the swirling image to the right.

Teach your eyes and mind to note conveyance—is it the vehicle by which all of our concepts and messages are delivered.

285

CONCEPT CONVEYANCE

On this page: one shoe and a pair of laces.

Opposite: the same elements, along with a dash of whimsy. Conveyance changes everything.

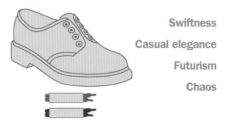

Swiftness

Casual elegance

Futurism

Chaos

Conveyance depends a lot on the person who is looking at the image or the layout being presented. Search for connotations—both visual and thematic—that will connect most directly with the target audience for your piece. (More on audiences beginning on page 329.)

287

Conveyances
can be added
together to
create new
conceptual
sums.

*Perhaps a graphic designer
who specializes in solutions
that are both creative and
practical could use an image
such as this as the basis for
a promotional postcard
or advertisement...*

CONVEYANCE

CONCEPT CONVEYANCE

289

LONELY AS CLOUD

Strive for thematic agreement between

subject matter, components and composition.

It's happening here.

Three's a crowd. A theme of disorderly merriment is conveyed through: 1) A sky jam-packed with toy air-planes; 2) Bold, multi-colored type that has been wedged into a tight-fit-ting block; and 3) Elements that overlap one another and leap gutters. **These composi-tional and content conven-tions make up a con-veyance of** *crowd,* *chaos* **and** *color.* **To help ensure a clear delivery of message, identify a word or set of words such as the ones above and use them as points-of-reference as you add elements and apply compositional and stylistic decisions to a layout.** For maximum effect, aim as many visual and thematic elements as possible toward a common conceptual goal.

[concordant connotations casting clear conveyances]

Each of the five images on this page carry a shared connotation of *energy*. Some of the photos convey *energy* in terms of electrical output or transmission; some in terms of movement.

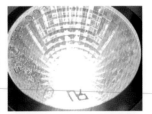

Being thus pointed toward the same thematic goal, these images make ideal components for a collage whose message is *energy*.

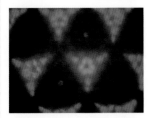

Note also the bitmapped typeface used in the collage itself. As a font with digital origins, it too carries energy-related conveyances that are in accord with the connotations delivered by the other elements.

When conveyances are in agreement, meaning is amplified.

Type can be used to impart play-ful conveyances of its own—either alongside or apart from the actual meaning(s) of the words being presented.

**A typographic joke.
Get it?**

Treatments such as these can raise the level of visual interest within a headline, logo or fea-tured typographic element.

**Meaning and
presentation jesting
with one another.**

**A typographic
"Escherism."**

**Type that means
what it says.**

An i, eye or both?

**Type and meaning
converge.**

CONVEYANCE

CONCEPT

Times Roman

green

un**q**pside

JUMP

s**p**lat

CONVEYANCE

CONCEPT CONVEYANCE

EXERCISE:

Connections.

Needed: paper, something to write with, graphics software.

Attention-grabbing logos and featured images are often made up of unexpected combinations between literal objects and conceptual conveyances. The logo for the bicycle delivery service at right illustrates such a connection. In this image, Mercury's helmeted, winged head has been subtly altered—here, the Greek god of speed and commerce wears a bike helmet rather than his usual metal cap.

The following exercise provides practice in a brainstorming technique that can be used to come up with intriguing visuals for all kinds of projects—from individual elements to entire layouts.

Here's your task: Design a logo for Maplewood Landscape Design that includes a visually and conceptually compelling graphic image—something out-of-the ordinary.

Try the following approach to search for a theme and design that are above and beyond the typical. On a large sheet of paper, make three columns—one for each of the three words in the company's name. These columns will be filled with nouns, verbs, adjectives and phrases related to each word. Now, add two more columns: one for words that are related to the thematic message(s) you want the logo to convey, and one that contains words and notes related to the stylistic presentation of the logo. Fill each column as completely as you can. Go for quantity—the more the better!

After you have established a strong set of words in each column, it's time to look for connections within and between them that spark your imagination toward a visually and thematically compelling logo design. Perhaps you'll find a combination between two different nouns that add up to an intriguing visual (as with the example on page 288), or maybe an adjective from one column will lead to an eye-catching image when applied to an object from another. Rule out nothing at this point—explore any and all avenues of creativity that have the slightest chance of leading to a solution. Remember: you are looking for out-of-the-ordinary solutions and it's usually easier to tame a wild notion than it is to pump energy into a lackluster idea. Make abundant notes and thumbnail sketches of potential solutions as you work (refer to "The Creative Process" beginning on page 321 for more brainstorm-related ideas). Don't follow any one idea too deeply at this point—concentrate on keeping your eyes and mind open to potential solutions for now—finalization can wait.

Don't stop brainstorming and sketching until you have at least a half-dozen viable and varied solutions for your logo. Once you have these, take two or three to presentation level using software and/or other design tools. Visually, apply everything you know about composition, typography and component-creation to your designs.

298

EXERCISE:

Typographic conveyance.

Needed: fonts, graphics software.

As shown on the previous spread, conveyances can be incorporated into typography to achieve intriguing visual effects.

Now it's your turn. Come up with a few typographic conveyances of your own using the list of words near the bottom of this column. Rules are few in this exercise; apply what you know about composition and typography, as well as concept and theme, to achieve type-based images that reflect the meaning of the word they portray.

Print your results, stand back and critique your designs. Make adjustments until you are satisfied with both the visual and conceptual result of your work.

Use words from this list or come up with your own for this exercise:

SHRED	BRICK
LIGHTLY	PILLOW
ATOM	XXL

Note: you may choose between upper- and lower-case (or a mix of both) for each word.

EXERCISE:

Observing conveyance.

Needed: senses.

It is said that we only use 5-10% our brain for conscious thought. Creating designs that speak only to this conscious, logical, literal portion of the viewer's brain is like trying to enter a coliseum through a cat door.

Conveyance speaks to the vast unconscious mind.

Conveyance is not logical.

Conveyance enters through the main gate.

Conveyance connects.

Great artists, working in all kinds of media, deliver meaning and emotion in ways that go far beyond the obvious and immediately recognized. Every consequential work of art, design, architecture, music and dance contains examples of conveyance at work.

Conveyance also happens on its own—the smell of a backyard barbeque, for example, conveys meaning and emotion, as do the rich colors of an autumn sunset or an empty park bench.

Become hypersensitive to the conveyances that occur around you in art, life and nature—*infuse your designs with conveyances that connect.*

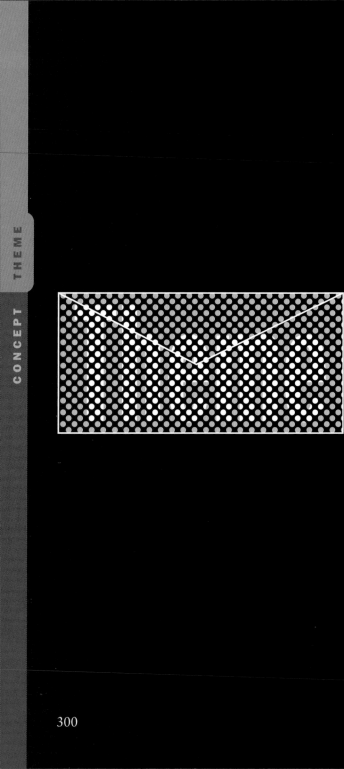

THEME

CONCEPT

300

Theme is the envelope in which concept is sent.

Theme is the tone of a piece, its emotional appeal (or lack thereof), its style of presentation.

The conveyances in the previous section deliver concept through themes of *organic growth, freeflowing creativity, swiftness, casual elegance, atomic futurism, tangled confusion, creative practicality, solitude, crowdedness, chaos, energy, mischief and humor.*

Theme is a powerful and influential force that speaks to the viewer on both conscious and subconscious levels.

Themes can be wonderfully enigmatic: *abstract but concrete, indefinable yet precise.*

If the theme of a piece is relevant and appealing to a viewer, and if each of the elements within the piece points toward that theme, connection with the viewer is maximized.

Theme can be applied to almost every project, from a business card to an ad campaign. Define the theme for your piece and write it down in its most distilled form—a word, a sentence. Keep this "thematic mission statement" before you as you work, and evaluate each element or idea that you add to the design against its ideals.

> **The following pages provide examples of broad thematic categories, as well as some means of delivering theme.**

How could you resist?

Most viewers are drawn to scenarios of warmth and welcome. Images and designs that convey these qualities can serve as people magnets—inviting attention and conveying affability.

Naturally, images such as this should also tie in with the overall message of the piece in which they are used. Once a viewer is drawn to investigate a design through a particular emotional appeal, they expect to find a message that is in accord with that theme. If they do not find this connection, they may feel manipulated and become distrustful of the piece's message.

And remember: theme is relative to audience. After all, if cats were people, how might they react to this photo?

EXERCISE:

Thematic agreement.

Needed: every hands-on and conceptual skill you possess.

Design a book cover for the following title: *Flirting with the Bully.*

Begin by deciding on a theme for your design. This theme could be exotic, pragmatic, playful, serious or poetic. It might be straightforward or enigmatic. You should be able to state your theme in a single word or a short sentence. Consider this theme carefully; it will direct the look-and-feel for every element of your design.

The design parameters for this project are wide open. You may use any kind of image, typographic element, compositional device and color scheme you like as long as each is aimed toward the same conceptual goal.

See how many thematic echoes you can achieve among the conceptual and visual elements of your layout. Look for ever deeper and more subtle ways of thematically enforcing the message of the design.

Come up with at least two presentation-ready layouts.

Strive for thematic agreement among every element of every design you create from now on.

303

Shock: it's mostly a matter of who the audience is and what they are used to seeing.

A grocery-store butcher is likely to see this image quite differently than a vegan activist.

Evaluate your audience and decide whether an unexpected or shocking theme might best serve the project. If so, brainstorm for content and presentation ideas.

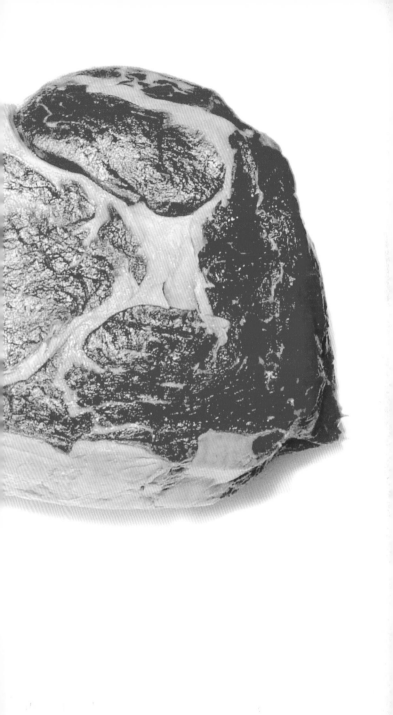

Missing You...

Themes can serious and contemplative. Themes can also be...

mischievous.

Coffee-shop woman taking a break behind the shop. Not exactly front page news, but still, there is a force at work here that's powerful enough to attract the attention of most viewers: the human element.

When we see people, both in real life and in pictures, we tend to "check them out"—especially those who we find attractive, intriguing or to whom we feel some kind of connection.

In many cases, adding a human element to a theme strengthens its appeal—as long as the people being featured are done so believably and in-tune with the target audience's tastes.

Clues about your audience's people-preferences can be found in books and magazines that are relevant and popular among these viewers. Additional intelligence might be gained through some actual field-work: observe members of your projected audience in their natural habitat—a mall, a bikers' bar, a nursing home, a fly-fishing convention—wherever they are likely to congregate.

The
theme
here is
obscure.
(Literally.)

Obscurity can be
used as a theme and as
a way of *delivering* theme.
Most people find it hard to
resist a well-presented puzzle,
actual or thematic. If this photo
were the featured image in an ad,
could you help yourself from reading at
least a line or two of the text to find out
what's going on?

Juxtaposition (a combination of objects that
seem to be at cross purposes or without an obvious
reason for their association) can be used to generate
intrigue, ambiguity and humor. Juxtaposition, when used
effectively, takes advantage of people's natural tendency to
investigate the deliciously obscure.

310

THEME

CONCEPT

Mischievous (and perhaps cynical) themes seem to be at play in this image. And even though its meaning is not immediately clear, the photo begs attention through a shameless appeal to the darkly capricious nature that abides in most of us.

Who knows, perhaps an image like this could be used to accompany an article on the pros and cons of long-term relationships, an exposé on co-dependency or the dangers of sexually transmitted diseases.

313

The good old days. Flashes from the past.

Many viewers find themselves drawn to themes of nostalgia whether or not they were ever a part of the era being alluded to.

The poster opposite is not an announcement from yesteryear, nor does it strive to pass itself off as one. Still, it contains visual references to days gone by: varied type styles, a muted palette and a crudely rendered illustration of an old-time country folk singer. Together, these stylistic clues infuse the poster with a hint of nostalgia.

If the audience for a particular message is one that might respond positively to this kind of presentation, consider your options and look to authentic samples from relevant eras for inspiration and ideas.

Should the instruction manual for a lawn mower be designed around themes of rage or sensuality? Probably not. Should a table of financial data contain thematic references of intrigue, spirituality or heavy metal rock-and-roll? Doubtful.

Utility and practicality are themes, too. And sometimes, they are the only themes that can be sensibly applied to a particular subject or project.

To carry off such a theme, each element of the design should point toward it through layout conventions that are straightforward, intelligible and clearly organized. In these cases, function and form become the standard of evaluation (as opposed to the more emotion-based criteria used in the previous thematic examples).

Still, that doesn't mean a designer can't throw in a surprise or two, even within austere themes. After all, themes are a lot like people; even the most serious folks have been known to crack a joke now and then.

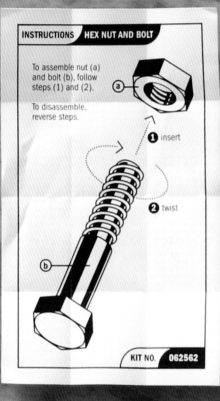

INSTRUCTIONS **HEX NUT AND BOLT**

To assemble nut (a) and bolt (b), follow steps (1) and (2).

To disassemble, reverse steps.

(a)

1 insert

2 twist

(b)

KIT NO. **062562**

VARIETY-WITHIN-UNITY

CONCEPT THEME

Variety-within-unity is the presentation of elements that are in accord with one another, and that also have a degree of individuality among them. And while not necessarily a theme itself, variety-within-unity is a principal that can be applied to all sorts of themes in order to to enrich and deepen their conceptual and aesthetic appeal.

Variety-within-unity has long been employed by artists working in all kinds of media.

The pattern at left is filled with a repetitive sequence of identical elements. As such, it provides apt decoration for the page. It is neither challenging to the viewer's eye nor particularly demanding of attention.

If the designer of a spread like this wanted to deepen the level of visual interest and energy of these pages, variations within the pattern could be sought.

318

The pattern at right is still based on the square-oriented theme of before, but variations have been applied to spice things up. While still relatively easy on the eye, this pattern also provides the viewer with subtle opportunities for visual exploration on both unconscious and conscious levels.

The degree to which you apply variation affects the energy and notice generated by a design or work of art. Greater variation usually results in greater measures of both energy and notice.

Don't be fooled by the simplicity of this demonstration. Variety-within-unity can be applied in endless degrees of subtlety and depth in all forms of art. Consider the structure of great musical pieces, the characters and plot of an intriguing story, the offerings of a fine meal, the components of a great painting, a typeface.

Variety-within-unity also exists abundantly in nature. Consider a field of poppies, waves coming ashore, the human race.

Wrap your head around this concept and you'll see examples of it everywhere in art and nature.

comme

working together

Building a layout is like building a tower of blocks.

The purpose of a tower is to...*tower*. **Right? Our** favorite block-towers seem to be those that reach high, stand securely, and tickle our aesthetic fancy.

To build such a tower, the blocks used must be selected in terms of fit, function and appearance (good block-tower-builders seem to know this instinctually). Every block of a great tower must be reaching toward one and the same goal: to rise, beautifully. Blocks that lie too far from the tower's center of balance, or ones that are colored or shaped in a way that visually conflicts with

ntary:

the others, put the sky-scraper's structural and visual integrity in jeopardy.

Back to layouts:

The purpose of a layout is to...*tower*. A successful layout stands above the status quo and delivers its message beautifully. The best layouts feature elements and attributes that share agreed-upon conceptual and aesthetic goals (goals that appropriately reflect both the needs of the audience and purpose of the piece).

Use instinct and logic to tell you whether each aspect and element of a design are working toward the delivery of the same message. Avoid adding elements that have a separate agenda, no matter how attractive they might be on their own. Develop an inner eye that looks for these relational dynamics as you work. Listen to the inner voice that tells you when you are on track and when you are beginning to stray.

Once you begin to look at your designs in this way, you'll begin to evaluate them in a whole new light.

Look around and you'll see: great layouts and works of art tend to be those whose elements point with the greatest degree of unison toward the most worthy goals.

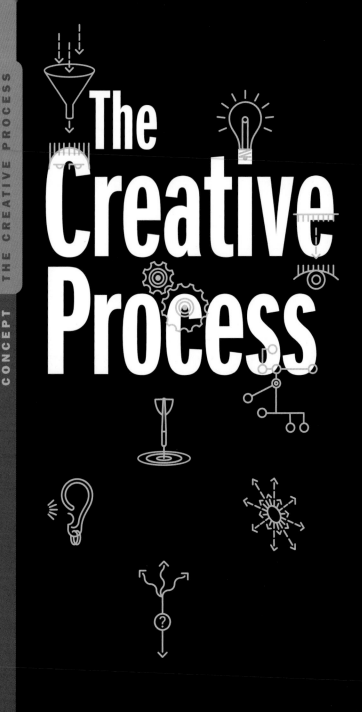

The Creative Process

There is no neutral state when it comes to creativity.

Anything that is alive and organically active is either growing or decaying. This is especially true of creativity (which, it could be argued, is itself an organic entity).

Observation, study, practice and play are all essential elements of creative growth. Each has to do with expanding our creativity through either nourishment or exercise.

Without a lively, flourishing array of instinctual and intellectual creative abilities, our hands-on technical skills are severely limited in what they can do for us.

Cultivating creativity often requires sweat and stamina, though it should not be seen as a chore or an obligation. (If it starts to feel that way, consider changing tactics or taking a vacation.)

Naturally, variances between artists' creative practices are endless. Therefore, the ideas and information in this section are offered as suggestions; fuel for thought. Look for ideas that square with your own, as well as those that are new to you and seem worthy of consideration. From there, create your own best ways of cultivating your imaginative and conceptual skills.

> In this chapter, we take a step backward. That is, we focus on the creative practices that stand *behind* the components and compositions through which our ideas take form.

YOUR OWN CREATIVE EXPANSION

Just as water cannot be released from a dam if the river behind it is dry, our creative output won't amount to much unless we are tapped in to a continuous source of fresh ideas and information.

Fill your creative reservoir by training your eyes to SEE and your brain to ABSORB. *Keep your eyes and brain with you at all times and keep them both wide open to input from without.*

Take the time to look at art (both commercial and fine). Look at the examples of architecture, fashion and advertising that come before your eyes each day. Look at automobiles and everyday objects of all sorts; take note of both their aesthetic and functional qualities. Look at people—closely. Look at faces, eyes, hands, elbows, feet. Look at the stuff that other people have put up on their walls. Look at handbills and graffiti. Look at environments, both natural and man-made. Go to libraries and bookstores (new and used) and look at books on art as well as books that have nothing to do with art. Visit galleries, visit museums. Take frequent field trips to places that feed creativity.

Strive to make *seeing* and *absorbing* the default settings for your eyes and mind.

Fill your creative reservoir from sources of all kinds: *Everything we allow to come into our conscious and unconscious mind can be used as creative fuel for all kinds of expression.*

Read. Read the classics, read pulp fiction, read a variety of magazines. Read before bed, read during lunch, read on the weekend. Read solo or as part of a group.

Watch movies that are not of the mainstream variety. Have you seen films by Akira Kurasawa? Sergei Eisenstein? Jean-Pierre Jeunet? Jim Jarmusch? Werner Herzog?

In addition to taking inspiration and information *in*, another essential activity for anyone who wants to expand their creative abilities is to put their ideas *out* there through the practice of their art(s).

Practice is an investment that yields great returns. For every idea that it borrows from our creative bank account, it adds two, three, tenfold in return.

Redefine "practice" as something you simply do, like breathing; not something you have to do, like cleaning the fish tank.

Practice what you are already good at. Practice what you want to do better. Suspend judgement when you practice; take chances. Save perfection for your professional and commercial work.

As artists and designers, most of us have always been doodlers and drawers. Who said we could stop doodling once we became "pros?" Keep something to draw with and something to draw on with you at all times. You can figure out a way to do this. *Every notebook that you fill with sketches and words leaves you a different artist than before.*

Invest in the tools necessary to create art. Don't be extravagant; modest tools suffice. Then again, don't be cheap—crummy tools can sometimes stand between what's in your head and what you are able to produce.

Practice digital skills as well. Take advantage of the powerful tools of the cyber-era to bring your personal visions to life. Create websites of your own, make digital movie shorts, alter photos and produce images from scratch.

How about experimenting with new media? Learn a musical instrument, borrow or buy a digital video camera, become a better cook, act. Creativity gained in one medium invariably spills over into others.

Get used to the idea that not everything you create will result in a monetary reward. Your after-hours and at-home art projects are for YOU, not for your client's benefit or your bank account.

All of these personal habits of observation, study and practice add significantly to our professional range of creative and hands-on skills.

PROFESSIONAL CREATIVITY

As commercial artists, we live something of a dual life. In our personal lives, we create for ourselves, our friends and for no one in particular. Professionally, we are asked to apply our creative abilities for the purposes of pleasing and meeting the needs of our bosses and our clients.

Our personal work is evaluated against terms of our own choosing—against what it is *we* want to accomplish or create. Our professional work, on the other hand, is

326

evaluated in terms of its ability to reach and deliver the client's message to a specific audience. Any professional project, if it is to succeed, must begin with an evaluation and understanding of the audience being targeted.

Concept may be King (and Queen, and Czar, etc.), but AUDIENCE is the force that governs over all.

When you get right down to it, we, as designers, are not being hired merely to create pretty designs and pictures. Designers are hired to create visuals that effectively deliver a specific message to a specific segment of the population (a.k.a., the "target" audience). Good designers are those who are able to consistently find ways of doing this. The thing that makes certain designers *great* is their ability to deliver well aimed messages that are also conceptually and aesthetically beautiful.

Identifying and understanding audience is an art unto itself. Many designers give short shrift to this essential aspect of professional creativity. This is a mistake. This means that the success or failure of their layouts will be more a matter of chance than design (pun intended).

Ask your client who they think the audience is for their project. What do they know about the likes and dislikes of these people? Is there a particular

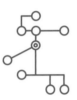

segment of their target audience that they wish to focus on? (This is important, since it is often impossible to speak to the entire spectrum of potential viewers.) Sometimes, conversations like this prove as useful to the client as they do to the designer—prompting new realizations for both.

Look at media that members of the target audience look at. It may not be media that you are familiar with. Learn the lingo, colors, fashions and trends embraced by the audience to whom you will be trying to connect. Add this perspective to your mindset as you work on your client's project.

Consider showing your preliminary ideas to people who represent the target audience. Get their feedback before moving ahead.

At the beginning of a project, strive to gain a true understanding of the audience you will be trying to reach (both in terms of aesthetic taste and emotional wants and needs). This way, your pathway to effective solutions will be far more direct than it would be if you were more or less groping in the dark for content that will connect with these viewers.

The needs and tastes of the audience should lie at the root of any design solution. Begin there and grow outward.

Once the AUDIENCE has been identified, the GOAL of a piece should be clearly defined.

The ultimate goal of most design projects are simply expansions of *"buy this product,"* or *"understand this information"* or *"consider this idea."*

Make sure that you and your client have a clear understanding of the goal(s) for any project before getting too far into the job. Work with the client to narrow the aim of their piece as much as possible. Most audiences have a short attention span: the more goals that an ad, brochure, website or poster tries to achieve, the less likely the audience is to pay attention to any of them.

> **An example of a reasonable, defined goal might sound something like this:** Convince prospective buyers that the advanced materials and technology used to build this mountain bike make it worth every penny of its upper-end price tag.

> **An example of a convoluted, difficult-to-reach goal might sound something like this:** Convince prospective buyers that the advanced materials, technology, wind-tunnel testing, flashy paint job, lifetime warranty and special rebate offer behind this mountain bike make it worth every penny of its high-end price tag and that it will turn heads every time you bring it out for a ride.

If the client simply has too much to say for a single ad or brochure, perhaps you could encourage them to run a series of ads or brochures instead.

Goals are like visual hierarchy (see "Emphasis," pages 62-77); it's usually best to grant dominance to one particular aim for a project. If there are other goals that must be included, make sure that they do not compete for attention with the primary objective.

When a piece's AUDIENCE has been identified and its GOAL defined, it's time to look for a MESSAGE that will achieve this goal.

Message is what you want to say to your audience through both the abstract conveyances and actual content of your layout or artwork.

Message can be delivered through many channels: words, typography, images, decoration, connotation, theme. A message is strongest when it is both enticing to its audience and when it is enforced, visually and thematically, by each element of a design.

At the beginning of a project, listen carefully to what your client has to say about the product or information they want to promote. Chances are, they know a lot more about it than you do at this point.

Take notes when you meet with a client! Record specifics about their product and its strengths. Get a handle on the language, both visual and textual, that is used to describe the product—this often provides the seeds from which headlines, text and visuals grow.

Ask the client what it is that could be seen as essential or desirable about their product (in the eyes of the audience being targeted). Ask what it is that sets this product apart from the crowd. Oftentimes, visual and thematic solutions for a project are contained in the client's answers to questions like these.

As you begin work on a project, strive to distill these "selling points" into a single, concise statement or directive. This guiding statement is meant for your personal, behind-the-scenes use and need not be polished; word it in whatever way works for you. Here are some examples:

This accounting software has more capabilities than the competition's and costs less to buy.

These new summer dresses are all about urban attitude and sass; not for the wallflower or happily married woman.

This 250cc off-road motorcycle is like a cross between a jet-fighter and Hummer.

Having established this thematic point-of-reference, use it to keep yourself on track as you move forward in search of specific concept, content and layout solutions that will best deliver the final message.

When a thematic direction is not established at or near the beginning of a project, focus tends to slide and broaden. When this happens, the final message tends to be blurred and tepid in its delivery.

Take note of the the media you see around you. Note the selling points that have been selected in order to promote a particular product. Note which designs seem to have the clearest message and the cleanest, most focused delivery. Also make a note of pieces whose elements seem to argue over what the overall message really is. Learn from both good and bad examples of message creation and delivery.

As far as actually delivering a visual and conceptual message to its intended audience, there are an infinite number of MEANS that could be employed.

Means are the specific words, colors, compositional devices, images, typefaces and (very importantly) stylistic conventions that we choose in order to bring our concepts to life.

Means make the invisible (concept, theme) visible (ad, business card, website). Means endow the abstract with substance and character.

Message is *what* you are saying; *means* is *how* you are saying it. When message and means converge, the concept's delivery is at peak strength.

As with *goal* and *message*, *means* should be evaluated against the needs and tastes of the audience.

When considering means, be sure to take your competition into account. What means have already been used to deliver similar messages to the targeted audience? What have these viewers already seen? What do you have to do to deliver this message in an original and effective way?

Ahead are strategies that can be used to come up with effective concepts, as well as means for delivering them.

BRAINSTORM

Everyone goes about the creative process differently.

Still, it's safe to say that most designers, most of the time, spend the early stages of a project exploring a wide range of ideas and approaches. This phase of a project should not be ignored or abbreviated; it's where most of the conceptual and visual components for the work ahead are hatched.

Brainstorming is the process of looking at many, many possible solutions for a project before narrowing the search to those few ideas that have the greatest potential for success.

Brainstorming is not always pretty (it's not called *storming* for nothing). Brainstorming should be short on rhyme and reason and long on havoc and fury. Brain-*storm*. There is an abundance of great ideas in the head of every designer, as well as a lot of ideas that that are merely good. To get at the great ones we have to be willing to shake things up, take chances and dig deep. (See "Be Different," pages 152-153.)

Focus is good when it comes to brainstorming, but so is peripheral vision. When searching for ideas, strive for a creative field-of-vision that is neither too narrow nor too broad. Develop a working "sweet spot" where you are able to focus on the pursuit of a specific idea while simultaneously allowing new thoughts and approaches to freely enter the fray.

When brainstorming, think, "Quantity now, quality later." Repeat this to yourself ten times before you begin cranking out the ideas... "quantity now, quality later; quantity now, quality later..."

When you brainstorm for concepts, conveyances and themes, you may want to write down words and phrases that point in the general direction of a solution. Make word-lists of nouns, verbs and adjectives that are related to potential content, theme or stylistic treatments for your project. As the list grows, look for interesting connections and combinations between the words. Word associations such as these often lead to both textual and visual solutions for a project.

Bring ideas from your head to paper by making quick sketches and doodles (often referred to as thumbnail sketches). Don't worry about neatness or finesse at this point. *Remember: quantity now, quality later.* The more thumbnails you record, the more material you will be able to sift through later on. If allowed, a kind of creative natural selection runs its course during this phase; the most fit and fertile ideas rise above the masses and await further evolution.

Brainstorm for all elements of a design, abstract and visual. Brainstorm for concepts, headlines, images, stylistic treatments, layout options—anything that might ultimately be a part of the final product.

Whenever possible, use large sheets of paper when brainstorming. *Big paper invites excess, encourages abandon.* Fill a page. Fill several. *Quantity now, quality later*!

During the initial stages of a project, it's also a good idea to look through relevant websites, books, magazines and trade publications for inspiring stylistic, content and presentational approaches. Note: In order to avoid being overly influenced by the work of others, many artists prefer to do this only after first sketching a satisfying quantity of their own ideas.

334

How will you know when you are done brainstorming and have enough potentially winning ideas to move ahead to further stages of refinement? Try asking yourself questions such as these:

Is there time for more brainstorming?

Have I explored a broad range of approaches (both in terms of style and content) or do my ideas look like variations of each other?

Within each germinating idea that I'm favoring, is every element pointed toward a common theme and message? Are these themes and messages pointed accurately toward the target audience?

Among promising thumbnails and preliminary layouts, is there anything that could be added or taken away to further improve their potential?

How do these ideas stack up against what is already out there? Have I come up with ideas that are different (and dare I say, better) than what other people have done?

What is my artistic gut-instinct saying about these ideas? Move forward? Explore some more? Try something really crazy? Should I take a break, stand back, and then decide?

Evaluating Concept

Put on your Evaluation C.A.P.

Thoroughly evaluate the concepts that provide the virtual framework for your layouts and designs. Look at them in terms of

CLARITY
AUDIENCE
PURPOSE

In addition to these three criteria, it is important to also judge your work using the C.A.P.'s related to Composition and Concept (pages 118-121 and 272-275).

1.
Clarity

Ask:

Are the literal, stylistic and thematic messages of this piece clearly and efficiently presented? **Is each working toward the same overall message and goal?** Is there any possibility for misinterpretation of the piece's message? **Is there more than one message fighting for attention here?** Could the concept, message or theme be simplified for the sake of impact?

2.

Audience

Ask:

Who is the target viewer for this piece? **Who does the client think their primary audience will be?** What are the visual tastes of this demographic segment? **What can you do to be sure of your conclusions?** What tone should the concept have if it is to be well-received by this audience? **What sort of lingo might they respond to?** What colors do they seem to prefer? **Does the concept behind this piece talk down to the target audience?** Might it fly over their heads? **What can this product or announcement provide that the audience wants, needs or desires?** Does this design stand apart from what this audience has already seen? **If this piece were a person, what would she/he look like and how would they behave?** What would the target audience think of this person?

3.
Purpose

Ask:

What exactly is this piece supposed to do? **Is it meant to sell a product?** If so, what particular aspect of this product is being promoted? **Is the purpose to inform or persuade?** If so, by what means? **Have you discussed the purpose with your client or art director?** Has the purpose of this piece been adequately narrowed so that it can be given as much attention and power as possible? **If not, what can be left out in favor of a more focused presentation?**

comme

portfolio

your

Whether you are looking for a job in an agency or going after a new client of your own, you've got to have a portfolio that shows people what you can do.

Up until recently, most portfolios were made up of 10-15 printed or rendered samples, presented in clear sleeves or mounted on pieces of mat board.

The cyber age has provided many new options for portfolio presentation. Web pages can be posted, PDFs sent, CDs distributed.

Your portfolio should not only show what you *can* do, it should also be aimed toward what you *want* to do next in your artistic life. That way, your samples are more likely to attract the kind of notice you want.

Do what you can to make your portfolio look different than anyone else's, without making it look showy or gimmicky.

If you have a broad range of capabilities and wish to highlight this fact, show a wide variety of samples. If you are more of a specialist, or if you wish to specialize in a particular area of design, then naturally, your portfolio should reflect this aptitude or desire.

ntary:

If your portfolio is portable—that is, if it is made up of actual, physical samples or images loaded onto a CD—take care to present its external packaging attractively. Presentation counts!

If your portfolio is on its own website, or part of another, make certain that it loads and functions properly on all major browsers and platforms. If someone goes to look at your site or page and has trouble viewing it, you lose.

Pay close attention to details like spelling and grammar within your portfolio and resume. Typos reflect very poorly on job-seekers in most any line of work.

If you are put in a situation where you have to sit there while someone else reviews your portfolio, stay calm. Just sit there and watch the process while trying to appear as comfortable and confident as you can. Don't worry about trying to explain your pieces unless invited to do so. Don't be surprised or offended if the reviewer spends less than 1.5 seconds looking at each sample (art directors are professionals and they are used to operating at high speed).

Opportunity strikes at unpredictable times; be prepared. When you are between jobs, or when work is slow, use that time to bring your portfolio up-to-date and, if it's time for a new look, give it a facelift.

PRINT/WEB

APPENDIX

Print/Web Appendix

As designers, most of our work ends up being repro-
duced as ink on paper or pixels on a screen. Therefore,
it is essential that we foster the technical know-how
needed to carry our ideas all the way from initial concept to their final printed or digital form.

Creative agencies prefer to hire and work with designers who understand the technical aspects of the media
for which they will be designing. This is because the
well-informed designer makes fewer time- and money-
wasting mistakes and requires less supervision than the
designer with a limited grasp of production realities.

Clients love designers who have a firm understanding
of today's printed and electronic media. These designers are able to get things done faster, cheaper and more
in line with pre-production expectations than their
unenlightened counterparts.

Printers and web programmers also enjoy working with
designers who have a solid and current understanding
of these media. There are few things as frustrating to a
printer or programmer than dealing with a designer
who does not know how to properly prepare their artwork for production.

It's very easy for designers in the ever-evolving digital era to fall
behind the times, but take heart: it's really not that hard to
keep up with the changes either. This section focuses on practical advice aimed toward helping designers gain an understanding of current technologies, as well as finding ways of
keeping up with the latest developments.

YOU AND TECHNOLOGY

The vast majority of today's designers use computers and software to create and compose their work. The state of the digital arts changes very rapidly—practically every month, new programs and new versions of old programs arrive on the scene.

Designers who want to be as commercially versatile and employable as possible must strive to keep abreast of these changes (and this, while simultaneously cultivating their purely creative skills). So, how can the creative-minded commercial artist of the cyber era keep up with the technology of their tools? Here are a couple of suggestions:

Focus on two or three software programs at first. If you are reasonably fluent in one vector-based program (Macromedia Freehand or Adobe Illustrator, for example) and and one pixel-based program (such as Adobe Photoshop or ACD Systems Canvas)* you will be able to cover a great deal of ground professionally. From there, gradually expand your know-how by learning additional programs that are relevant to the work you do (or the work you *want to be doing instead*). This might include software aimed toward electronic publishing, web development, animation, illustration, photo-enhancement, 3-D rendering, book publication or digital movie-making.

346

Here's another easy practice that you can employ to help stay informed of events and info surrounding your trade: look through at least two current computer-related magazines every month. There are numerous periodicals devoted to late-breaking Mac and PC news (some with more design-oriented content with others). Not only does this habit help keep you apprised of the big picture in the digital world, it also provides you with a flow of tips and techniques that you can apply to your daily work.

YOU AND REAL-WORLD PRINTING

Printing companies have it hard. First, they are are forced to take artwork from designers who may or may not understand the printing process. And then, from this artwork, they are expected to produce ink-on-paper documents that meet the expectations (realistic or otherwise) of the designer and the designer's client!

*Most digital artwork is created using either vector-based or pixel-based graphics software. In short, **vector-based** programs are those that use mathematical formulas to define lines, curves, gradations and type elements in such a way that their products can be output at virtually any size with no loss of quality. These programs are ideal for the creation of logos and images that are made up of linework and relatively basic fills and gradations. Freehand and Illustrator are two powerful and popular vector-based programs. **Pixel-based** programs such as Photoshop are ideal for working with photographs and other images that contain more complex and varied shading. When using pixel-based software, the designer or illustrator must always take image-resolution into account. Higher resolution allows for more detail but results in larger file sizes and makes greater demands on the computer.

You can make life a lot easier for printing companies—as well as for yourself and your client—by learning everything you can about what is needed to translate your layouts and ideas into print-ready documents. After all, what good are spectacular creative skills to a designer who does not know how to get their creations printed accurately and within budget?

The best way to learn about printing is to talk with printing professionals. Show your printer electronic or paper layouts of the job(s) you are working on and ask them how they would like to have the artwork prepared. Ask if they see any areas of concern, or simple ways that the artwork might be altered in order to save on production costs. Make a habit of doing this early on in the production process. That way you will avoid many blood-pressure-raising experiences (for you, the client and the printer) when the job goes to press.

Read books on printing and pre-press strategies and skills. (*Pre-press* is the work done to prepare digital and traditional artwork for the printing process.) The more you know about the world of printing and pre-press, the better you will be at designing pieces that, when printed, stand the best chance of fulfilling the expectations of your client and yourself.

In addition to sharpening your knowledge of the printing process, also take seriously your role as an intermediary between printer and client. As the designer on a project, you are often the only bridge between these two parties. It's up to you to make sure that the client understands issues surrounding print realities such as timelines, differences between proofs and actual printed material and payment obligations. Nearly all print-related mistakes and disappointments are the result of inadequate communication between designer, client and printer. Therefore, make every effort to keep all participants in the printing process informed and up-to-speed. If *you* don't do this, there's no guarantee that anyone else will.

YOU AND THE WEB

Ever-increasing connection speeds, as well as ever-faster computers, mean that web designers are able to offer content that is more and more digitally complex and demanding. It also means that the software and technologies used to create electronic content is in a constant and rapid state of flux.

Freelancers who do web work need a good set of both artistic and technical skills to handle the full scope of the jobs that are likely to come their way. Designers working within an agency environment are often able to focus on the artistic aspects of web development since the technical responsibilities are commonly handled by specialists in other departments. In either case, just as with print media, the more a designer knows about how their work will actually be produced, the better they will be at find-ing trouble-free paths between conception and construc-tion.

Keeping up with technology in this arena means staying current on the latest trends and developments. And, again, this need not be a hideous challenge to the busy artist or designer. Simply allow a reasonable amount of time to devote to magazines and books about computers and web development. Also, consider attending seminars and computer-user groups as a way of networking with like-minded professionals.

If there is a particular area of web development that you would like to focus on or specialize in, consider taking classes or self-educating yourself for a certain amount of time. This may mean a cut in pay (or free time) for a while, but it may also lead to an increase in salary and employability in the future. Talk to professionals in the industry to get an idea of what technologies seem to be on the rise and where your efforts could be most productively applied.

YOU AND THE FUTURE

It's easy to feel intimidated by the rapid advancements in digital technology, but take heart: coping with the changes is easier than it might seem at first.

350

Consider this: it could be argued that painters and draftspersons of yesteryear had to climb a much steeper learning curve on their way to proficiency than digital artists of today. The time-investment demanded by "traditional" tools such as paint, ink pens and t-squares, is as great (and probably greater) than that which is required to learn most new software programs. Furthermore, as software programs evolve, so too does the intuitive nature of their interfaces—making them bulk of them easier to learn, use and master.

It is also important to remember that creativity itself hasn't changed at all over the years. Originality is still original, and communication is still the goal of nearly everything we do as designers and artists. Cultivating creativity in ourselves is as important today as always; and it's no harder or easier than ever before.

So then, what does the present day designer do in order to succeed in the world of commercial art? Same thing as always: foster personal creativity, learn the language of aesthetics and strive for proficiency with the tools of their trade.

Design well, enjoy yourself and thanks for reading.

Jim Krause

INDEX

More great titles from Jim Krause!

Inside this pocket-sized powerhouse you'll discover thousands of ideas for graphic effects and type treatments—via hundreds of prompts designed to stimulate and expand your creative thinking. Use *Idea Index* to brainstorm ideas, explore different approaches to your work and stir up some creative genius when you need it most.

ISBN 1-58180-046-0, paperback w/vinyl cover, 312 pages

Break through design dilemmas to create eye-catching layouts with ease. Inside *Layout Index* you'll find hundreds of visual and written idea generators for bold graphics and creative solutions, no matter what your layout challenge. Consider it your secret weapon for designing stunning brochures, ads, web pages, stationery, posters, flyers and more.

ISBN 1-58180-146-7, paperback w/vinyl cover, 312 pages

This definitive graphic design guide on color provides more than one thousand color combinations and formulas—guaranteed to help you solve design dilemmas and create effective images for both print and the web. With *Color Index*, you will start working with color in exciting new ways and create original, eye-catching designs that will pop off the page.

US ISBN 1-58180-236-6
UK ISBN 0-7153-1397-5
paperback w/vinyl cover, 360 pages

Navigate through a playful collection of rock-solid advice, thought-provoking concepts, and suggestions and exercises designed to stimulate the creative, innovative thinking you need to do your job well. *Creative Sparks* will show you how to find inspiration in the world around you, spark new ideas, and act as a guide to your unique creative path.

US ISBN 1-58180-438-5
UK ISBN 0-7153-1735-0
hardcover, 312 pages

These books and other fine titles are available from your local bookstore, online supplier or by calling 1-800-448-0915 in North America or 0870-2200220 in the UK.

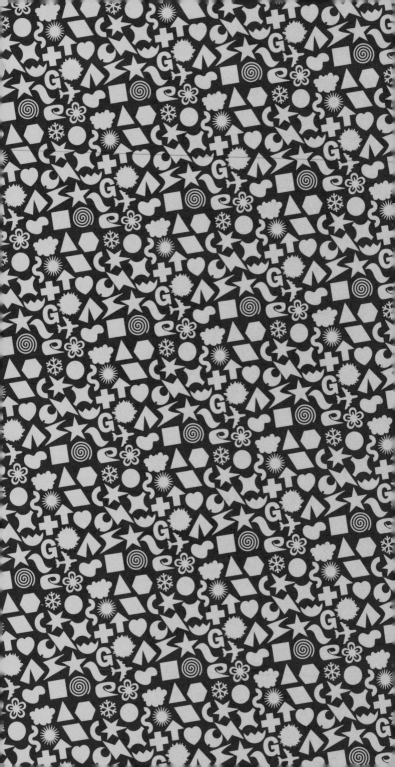